STATE AND LOCAL POLICY INITIATIVES TO REDUCE HEALTH DISPARITIES

Workshop Summary

Karen M. Anderson, *Rapporteur*

Roundtable on the Promotion of Health Equity and the Elimination of Health Disparities

Board on Population Health and Public Health Practice

INSTITUTE OF MEDICINE
OF THE NATIONAL ACADEMIES

THE NATIONAL ACADEMIES PRESS
Washington, D.C.
www.nap.edu

THE NATIONAL ACADEMIES PRESS   500 Fifth Street, N.W.   Washington, DC 20001

NOTICE: The project that is the subject of this report was approved by the Governing Board of the National Research Council, whose members are drawn from the councils of the National Academy of Sciences, the National Academy of Engineering, and the Institute of Medicine. The members of the committee responsible for the report were chosen for their special competences and with regard for appropriate balance.

This project was supported by contracts between the National Academy of Sciences and the Centers for Disease Control and Prevention (200-2005-13434); Sanofi-aventis (B09-39223); The California Endowment (20052634); Missouri Foundation for Health (08-0006-HPC-08); Connecticut Health Foundation (unnumbered); Merck and Co., Inc. (unnumbered); United Health Foundation (unnumbered); and Kaiser Permanente. Any opinions, findings, conclusions, or recommendations expressed in this publication are those of the author(s) and do not necessarily reflect the view of the organizations or agencies that provided support for this project.

This summary is based on the proceedings of a workshop that was sponsored by the Roundtable on the Promotion of Health Equity and the Elimination of Health Disparities. It is prepared in the form of a workshop summary by and in the name of the rapporteur as an individually authored document.

International Standard Book Number-13: 978-0-309-18745-9
International Standard Book Number-10: 0-309-18745-1

Additional copies of this report are available from the National Academies Press, 500 Fifth Street, N.W., Lockbox 285, Washington, DC 20055; (800) 624-6242 or (202) 334-3313 (in the Washington metropolitan area); Internet, http://www.nap.edu.

For more information about the Institute of Medicine, visit the IOM home page at, **www.iom.edu**.

Copyright 2011 by the National Academy of Sciences. All rights reserved.

Printed in the United States of America.

The serpent has been a symbol of long life, healing, and knowledge among almost all cultures and religions since the beginning of recorded history. The serpent adopted as a logotype by the Institute of Medicine is a relief carving from ancient Greece, now held by the Staatliche Museen in Berlin.

Suggested citation: IOM (Institute of Medicine). 2011. *State and Local Policy Initiatives to Reduce Health Disparities: Workshop Summary.* Washington, DC: The National Academies Press.

*"Knowing is not enough; we must apply.
Willing is not enough; we must do."*
—Goethe

INSTITUTE OF MEDICINE
OF THE NATIONAL ACADEMIES

Advising the Nation. Improving Health.

THE NATIONAL ACADEMIES
Advisers to the Nation on Science, Engineering, and Medicine

The **National Academy of Sciences** is a private, nonprofit, self-perpetuating society of distinguished scholars engaged in scientific and engineering research, dedicated to the furtherance of science and technology and to their use for the general welfare. Upon the authority of the charter granted to it by the Congress in 1863, the Academy has a mandate that requires it to advise the federal government on scientific and technical matters. Dr. Ralph J. Cicerone is president of the National Academy of Sciences.

The **National Academy of Engineering** was established in 1964, under the charter of the National Academy of Sciences, as a parallel organization of outstanding engineers. It is autonomous in its administration and in the selection of its members, sharing with the National Academy of Sciences the responsibility for advising the federal government. The National Academy of Engineering also sponsors engineering programs aimed at meeting national needs, encourages education and research, and recognizes the superior achievements of engineers. Dr. Charles M. Vest is president of the National Academy of Engineering.

The **Institute of Medicine** was established in 1970 by the National Academy of Sciences to secure the services of eminent members of appropriate professions in the examination of policy matters pertaining to the health of the public. The Institute acts under the responsibility given to the National Academy of Sciences by its congressional charter to be an adviser to the federal government and, upon its own initiative, to identify issues of medical care, research, and education. Dr. Harvey V. Fineberg is president of the Institute of Medicine.

The **National Research Council** was organized by the National Academy of Sciences in 1916 to associate the broad community of science and technology with the Academy's purposes of furthering knowledge and advising the federal government. Functioning in accordance with general policies determined by the Academy, the Council has become the principal operating agency of both the National Academy of Sciences and the National Academy of Engineering in providing services to the government, the public, and the scientific and engineering communities. The Council is administered jointly by both Academies and the Institute of Medicine. Dr. Ralph J. Cicerone and Dr. Charles M. Vest are chair and vice chair, respectively, of the National Research Council.

www.national-academies.org

MEMBERS OF THE PLANNING COMMITTEE[1]

NICOLE LURIE[2] (*Chair*), The RAND Corporation, Arlington, VA
TOM GRANATIR, Humana, Inc., Chicago, IL
CARA V. JAMES, Henry J. Kaiser Family Foundation, Washington, DC
DAVID P. PRYOR, Aetna, Inc., Thousand Oaks, CA
MILDRED THOMPSON, PolicyLink, Oakland, CA

---

[1] Institute of Medicine planning committees are solely responsible for organizing the workshop, identifying topics, and choosing speakers. The responsibility for the published workshop summary rests with the workshop rapporteur and the Institute of Medicine.

[2] Resigned June 2009.

MEMBERS OF THE ROUNDTABLE ON THE PROMOTION OF HEALTH EQUITY AND THE ELIMINATION OF HEALTH DISPARITIES[1]

NICOLE LURIE[2] (*Chair*), The RAND Corporation, Arlington, VA
WILLIAM VEGA[3] (*Chair*), Professor, University of California, Los Angeles
MILDRED THOMPSON (*Cochair*), Senior Director, PolicyLink
PATRICIA BAKER, President and Chief Executive Officer, The Connecticut Health Foundation
ANNE C. BEAL, President, Aetna Foundation
AMERICA BRACHO, Chief Executive Officer, Latino Health Access
FRANCIS D. CHESLEY, Director, Office of Extramural Research, Education, and Priority Populations, Agency for Healthcare Research and Quality
JAMILA DAVISON, Instructor, Emory University
ALLAN GOLDBERG, Executive Director, Science Affairs Cardiovascular/Metabolic Business Unit, U.S. Pharmaceuticals, Merck & Co., Inc.
GARTH N. GRAHAM, Deputy Assistant Secretary for Minority Health, U.S. Department of Health and Human Services
TOM GRANATIR, Director, Policy and Research, Humana, Inc.
CARA V. JAMES, Senior Policy Analyst, Henry J. Kaiser Family Foundation
JENNIE R. JOE, Professor, Department Family and Community Medicine, and Director, Native American Research and Training Center, University of Arizona
JAMES R. KIMMEY, President and Chief Executive Officer, Missouri Foundation for Health
JAMES KRIEGER, Chief, Chronic Disease and Injury Prevention Section, Seattle King County Health Department
ANNE C. KUBISCH, Codirector, The Aspen Institute
JEFFREY LEVI, Executive Director, Trust for America's Health
JOHN LEWIN, Chief Executive Officer, American College of Cardiology
NEWELL McELWEE, Executive Director, U.S. Outcomes Research, Merck & Co., Inc.
GARY D. NELSON, President, Healthcare Georgia Foundation

---

[1] Institute of Medicine forums and roundtables do not issue, review, or approve individual documents. The responsibility for the published workshop summary rests with the workshop rapporteur and the Institute of Medicine.
[2] Resigned June 2009.
[3] Chair since October 2009.

ELENA O. NIGHTINGALE, Scholar in Residence, Institute of Medicine
SAMUEL NUSSBAUM, Executive Vice President and Chief Medical Officer, WellPoint, Inc.
TERRI PEDONE, Director, Sanofi-Aventis
DAVID P. PRYOR, Medical Director, Aetna, Inc.
STEVE M. PU, General Surgeon, Missouri Foundation for Health
AMELIE G. RAMIREZ, Director, Institute for Health Promotion Research
KYU RHEE, Chief Medical Officer, Health and Human Services
JOY SMITH, Executive Director, National Association of State Offices of Minority Health
SAMUEL SO, Lui Hac Minh Professor, Stanford University
PATTIE TUCKER, Lead Health Scientist, Centers for Disease Control and Prevention
SID VOORAKKARA, Program Officer, The California Endowment
WINSTON F. WONG, Medical Director, Community Benefit, and Director, Disparities Improvement and Quality Initiatives, Kaiser Permanente
TERRI D. WRIGHT, Program Director, Health Policy, W. K. Kellogg Foundation

Study Staff

KAREN M. ANDERSON, Senior Program Officer
ROSE MARIE MARTINEZ, Director, Board on Population Health and Public Health Practice
PAMELA A. LIGHTER, Senior Program Assistant (*until January 2011*)
COLIN F. FINK, Senior Program Assistant (*after January 2011*)
PATRICK BURKE, Financial Officer (*October 2008 through October 2009*)
AMY M. PRZYBOCKI, Financial Officer (*November 2009 to present*)
HOPE HARE, Administrative Assistant

Reviewers

This report has been reviewed in draft form by individuals chosen for their diverse perspectives and technical expertise, in accordance with procedures approved by the National Research Council's Report Review Committee. The purpose of this independent review is to provide candid and critical comments that will assist the institution in making its published report as sound as possible and to ensure that the report meets institutional standards for objectivity, evidence, and responsiveness to the study charge. The review comments and draft manuscript remain confidential to protect the integrity of the deliberative process. We wish to thank the following individuals for their review of this report:

Meredith Benedict, Anthurium Solutions, Inc.
Jamila Davison, Emory University
Steve M. Pu, Missouri Foundation for Health
Pattie Tucker, Centers for Disease Control and Prevention

Although the reviewers listed above have provided many constructive comments and suggestions, they were not asked to endorse the conclusions or recommendations nor did they see the final draft of the report before its release. The review of this report was overseen by **Antonia M. Villarruel**. Appointed by the National Research Council, she was responsible for making certain that an independent examination of this report was carried out in accordance with institutional procedures and that all review comments were carefully considered. Responsibility for the final content of this report rests entirely with the authoring committee and the institution.

Contents

1 INTRODUCTION 1
   Scope of the Workshop, 2
   Workshop Agenda, 2
   Key Themes, 3
   Organization of the Report, 4

2 CHANGING THE CONDITIONS OF COMMUNITIES
   WHERE PEOPLE LIVE 5
   Using Data to Document Health Disparities, 5
   The Two Steps Back Framework, 9
   Specific Recommendations, 11
   Discussion, 12
   References, 13

3 THE PHILLIPS-POWDERHORN EXPERIENCE AND THE
   ALLINA BACKYARD PROJECT 15
   Mayor R. T. Rybak, 15
   Discussion, 17
   Gordon Sprenger, 19
   Richard Pettingill, 21
   Sanne Magnan, 24
      Health Care Reform Efforts, 24
      Eliminating Health Disparities Initiative Efforts and
         Priorities in Minnesota, 25
      Working with Policy Makers, 26

Discussion and Questions, 27
References, 31

4 HEALTH DISPARITIES IN GREAT BRITAIN AND
  MASSACHUSETTS: POLICY SOLUTIONS   33
    The Health Care System in England, 33
    National Support Teams: Emerging Themes from the
      Infant Mortality Support Team Visits, 36
    Discussion, 40
    Health Disparity-Related Activities Under Massachusetts
      Health Care Reform, 40
      Chapter 58: Massachusetts Health Care Reform, 40
      Will Universal Coverage Lead to Reductions in Disparities?, 41
      Disparities Provisions in Chapter 58, 42
      Pay-for-Performance Approaches, 44
      Conclusions, 46
    Discussion, 46
    References, 46

5   REACTOR PANEL   47
    Brian Smedley, 47
    Winston Wong, 48
    Atum Azzahir, 50
    Questions and Discussion, 52
    Closing Comments, 55
    References, 57

Appendixes
A   A TIME OF OPPORTUNITY: LOCAL SOLUTIONS TO
    REDUCE INEQUITIES IN HEALTH AND SAFETY   59
B   AGENDA   115
C   SPEAKER BIOGRAPHICAL SKETCHES   119

1

Introduction

Although some attention is paid to the reduction of health disparities at the national level, information about successful efforts at the state and local levels is seldom heard. What are the policy levers that have led to successful state or local initiatives? To make progress at the national level, it is important to understand what has worked at other levels of government.

Similarly, successes in other nations might provide important lessons for the United States. For example, what is going on with health inequalities in England, where there is clear accountability and strong support for reducing health disparities?

The present workshop, then, was designed to focus on state and local policy initiatives to improve health disparities. The workshop also included information about efforts at reducing health disparities in England. There, health officials carefully look at the data to identify the drivers of health disparities. Once this has occurred, they then figure out who is responsible and who has leverage over those issues and then get local agencies to work together.

This workshop follows four earlier workshops convened by the Roundtable on the Promotion of Health Equity and the Elimination of Health Disparities. The first, held in St. Louis, Missouri, focused on the interface between the health care system and the community in which it is based. The second, held in Atlanta, Georgia, looked at issues of disparities across the life span, with a particular emphasis on young children. The third, held in Newport Beach, California, drew on the potential linkages between health literacy, health disparities, and quality improvement efforts. Finally, the fourth one, held in Los Angeles, California, investigated the role of

1

framing in addressing health disparities and the impact that the nation's demographic changes are having on health disparities.

The purpose of the Roundtable is to convene various groups of people and continue to have a dialogue. As a Roundtable is not a formal Institute of Medicine committee, the members do not make recommendations. Workshops serve as a way to present and disseminate ideas to a broader audience of people, including policy makers, government agency staff, members of the health care workforce, and interested participants from the general public.

SCOPE OF THE WORKSHOP

On May 11, 2009, the Institute of Medicine's Roundtable on the Promotion of Health Equity and the Elimination of Health Disparities sponsored a public workshop to discuss the role of state and local policy initiatives in reducing health disparities. With the advent of health care reform at the federal level, it is all the more important that ways of reducing existing disparities and promoting health equity at the state and local levels be examined. Institutional policies, such as those created by health plans, should also be studied in conjunction with state and local concerns. In this summary, information about policies to reduce disparities within Kaiser Permamente and Allina Health System is also presented.

The workshop, entitled State and Local Policy Initiatives to Reduce Health Disparities, was organized to look beyond federal initiatives to the state and local levels to learn more about what works. The hope is to advance the dialogue about health disparities by facilitating discussion among stakeholders in the community, academia, health care professions, business, policy-making entities, and philanthropic organizations. The goal of the meeting was to discuss how to highlight the importance of "community" when ways to address health disparities are addressed. A focus on several different geographic areas could help identify commonalities in community strategies, best practices, and lessons learned from community successes and failures in addressing health disparities.

WORKSHOP AGENDA

The workshop began with the presentation of a paper commissioned by the Roundtable and authored by Larry Cohen, Rachel Davis, and Sharon Rodriguez of the Prevention Institute and Anthony Iton of the Alameda County Department of Public Health. Their paper, A Time for Opportunity: Local Solutions to Reduce Inequities in Health and Safety, outlines several dozen recommendations for reducing health disparities and promoting health equity at the local level. The full version of the paper can be found in Appendix A.

The participants spent the rest of the morning hearing more about efforts being undertaken in Minneapolis, Minnesota, in particular and in the state of Minnesota in general. Minneapolis Mayor R. T. Rybak spoke about the changes taking place in Minneapolis at the community level, including efforts to create more affordable housing and supporting a local food movement. Gordon Sprenger, former chief executive officer of Allina Health Systems, gave the history of the development of the Allina Backyard Project, an ambitious neighborhood-based program designed to create jobs and incorporate other structural changes into a plan to reduce health disparities. The final speaker of that morning, Sanne Magnan, who is the Commissioner of Health in Minnesota, presented data on health disparities at the state level and described plans being undertaken statewide to improve health equity.

The afternoon sessions presented additional discussions of efforts at the state level as well as those at the national level in England. Annette Williamson of the Department of Health in England described the National Support Teams program, designed specifically to reduce infant mortality rates across that country. Although England has national health goals, the support teams at the local level can determine how best to meet those goals in their communities. Joel Weissman of the Executive Office of Health and Human Services in the Commonwealth of Massachusetts spoke about how state-level reforms have affected health disparities.

The day concluded with reactions to the earlier presentations by a three-member panel: Winston Wong of Kaiser Permanente, Brian Smedley from the Joint Center for Political and Economic Studies, and Atum Azzahir of the Phillips-Powderhorn Cultural Wellness Center. These individuals shared their perceptions of the information presented throughout the day. Following this panel, Nicole Lurie, chair of the Roundtable, offered concluding remarks.

The following is a summary of the presentations and discussions at the workshop and as such is limited to the views presented and discussed during the workshop. The broader scope of issues pertaining to this subject area is recognized but could not be addressed in this summary. Appendix B provides the workshop agenda, and Appendix C presents biographical sketches of all workshop presenters.

KEY THEMES

Throughout the workshop, speakers, and workshop participants highlighted several recurring themes:

- Residential segregation. Gentrification, urban renewal, and the historical practice of redlining (refusing to lend money to borrowers based upon race or refusing to lend money to purchase housing in an area with a high concentration of minorities) all affect where low-income people of color can live. This, in turn, affects their health.
- Race and racism. Race interacts with the process of residential segregation and thus cannot be ignored when health outcomes are evaluated.
- Lack of access to health care. Lack of access, especially for specialty care, is a major problem for people of color living in low-income communities.
- Lack of community infrastructure. A lack of safe places to walk and exercise and a lack of access to large grocery stores in a community affect the health of the residents in that community. These are important because skyrocketing obesity rates in some racial and ethnic minority groups are contributing to rising rates of chronic diseases, such as diabetes, which can be ameliorated by exercise and a healthy diet.
- Other community factors. Poverty and violence are major contributors to racial and ethnic health disparities.
- Shorter life spans for future generations. Several speakers noted that if current trends continue, children born today will not live as long as their parents do. Studies of foreign-born immigrant children and U.S.-born children of immigrant parents indicate that the U.S.-born children will have shorter life spans than their parents.

ORGANIZATION OF THE REPORT

The report that follows summarizes the presentations and discussions that occurred during the workshop.

Chapter 2 reviews the presentation and discussion of the commissioned paper, A Time for Opportunity: Local Solutions to Reduce Inequities in Health and Safety. Chapter 3 describes the efforts made to reduce health disparities at the local level in Minneapolis and at the state level in Minnesota.

Chapter 4 includes a set of introductory comments from Roundtable member Tom Granatir, followed by Annette Williamson's presentation about efforts in England. Joel Weissman's observations about the effects of health care reform at the state level follow. Finally, Chapter 5 describes the comments and observations of the reactor panel and the concluding comments of the Roundtable chair, Nicole Lurie.

2

Changing the Conditions of Communities Where People Live

Three of the four coauthors of the paper commissioned by the Roundtable, A Time for Opportunity: Local Solutions to Reduce Inequities in Health and Safety, Tony Iton, Rachel Davis, and Larry Cohen, each presented descriptions of different aspects of the paper (the full text of the paper can be found in Appendix A). The three presentations were followed by questions and discussion with members of the Roundtable and workshop participants.

USING DATA TO DOCUMENT HEALTH DISPARITIES

Tony Iton spoke of the importance of having data to document the role of social determinants in health status. The availability of data allows the correlations between policies, institutional practices, and health disparities to be examined.

Death certificates are among the most comprehensive data sets available to public health researchers. For example, in California a death is not officially recorded until the local registrar of vital records, the county health officer signs the death certificate. Death certificates contain a great deal of useful information for researchers, including cause of death, age at death, race/ethnicity, and place of residence. These data reveal a narrative about the distribution of life and death across a community (Alameda County Public Health Department, 2008).

Iton used the data from over 400,000 death certificates from over a 45-year period in Alameda County, California, and compared life expectancies for whites and blacks. In 1960, whites had a life expectancy that

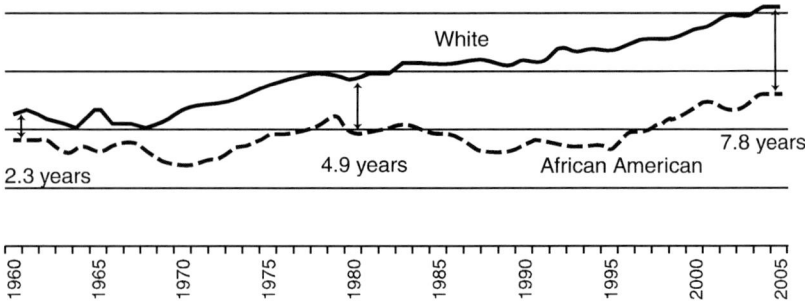

FIGURE 2-1 Health inequities by race and ethnicity in Alameda County, California.

was longer by about 2½ years. By 1980, that difference had doubled to a life expectancy that was almost 5 years longer for whites than for blacks. By 2005, that life expectancy difference had increased to nearly 8 years (Figure 2-1).

These data can also be mapped geographically according to where the premature deaths cluster at the county level. Looking again at the data from Alameda County, the neighborhoods with the longest average life expectancies (census tracts depicted in green) also had high rates of high school graduation, low rates of unemployment, relatively low rates of poverty, and high rates of home ownership. In Alameda County, neighborhoods with long life expectancies are about 50 percent white and 50 percent nonwhite (Figure 2-2).

Figure 2-3 shows that the neighborhoods with a middle to long average life expectancy (census tracts depicted in yellow) have relatively high rates of high school graduation (81 percent) and low rates of unemployment, and about half the residents of this census tract are homeowners. This area is slightly less diverse, at nearly 60 percent nonwhite.

Figure 2-4 shows the neighborhoods in the county with the shortest average life expectancy (census tracts depicted in red). These neighborhoods also have relatively low rates of high school graduation and higher rates of unemployment, 25 percent of the residents live in poverty, and 90 percent of the residents are nonwhite. The West Oakland neighborhood pictured in Figure 2-4 reveals a heavily industrial area adjacent to a residential area.

By mapping census tract data showing poverty levels on top of these data, it is possible to conduct a simple bivariate analysis (looking at life expectancy on one axis and poverty on the other axis). This is what Iton calls "the true poverty tax." This shows the true cost of being poor measured as the likelihood of premature death in Alameda County. Every level of income has a corresponding average life expectancy. In other words,

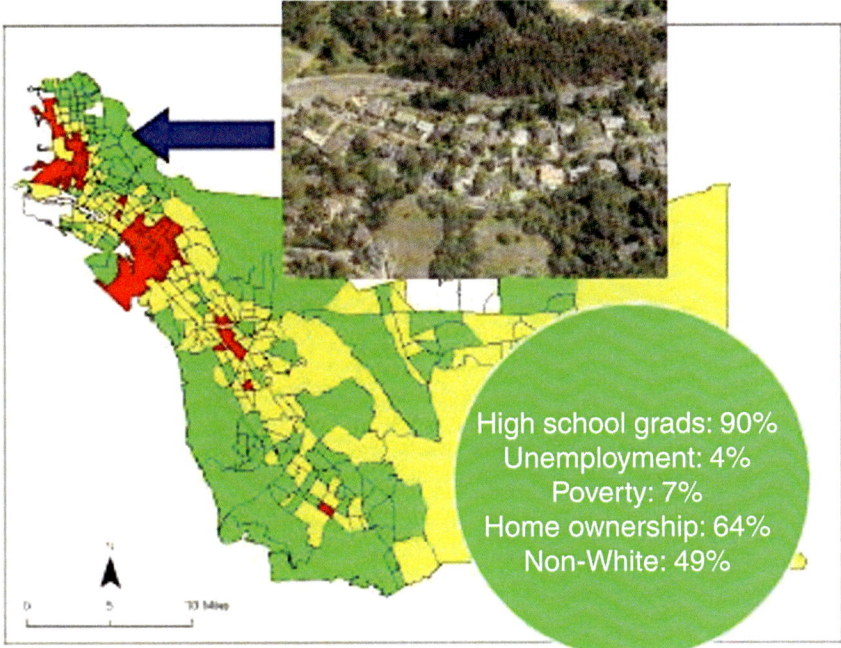

FIGURE 2-2 Neighborhoods in Alameda County with the longest average life expectancy.

income is a fairly good predictor of how long a person will live, because every level of income has a corresponding average life expectancy. This phenomenon holds not just for the poor, but also for the middle class.

In the San Francisco Bay Area of Northern California, Iton calculated that $12,500 buys an additional year of life. This so-called social gradient allows one to calculate the cost of a year of life in many U.S. communities, including New York City, Philadelphia, Cleveland, Los Angeles, Minneapolis–St. Paul, and Baltimore. In Baltimore, $10,000 buys an additional 3 years of life.

Using the Alameda County data, Iton and his colleagues in the county (Alameda County Public Health Department, 2008) produced a report concluding that the most important drivers of the differences in life expectancies were not related to access to health care. Rather, the social determinants of health lead to differences in life expectancy and other important health outcomes. How poor a person is should not determine how long that person lives.

8   POLICY INITIATIVES TO REDUCE HEALTH DISPARITIES

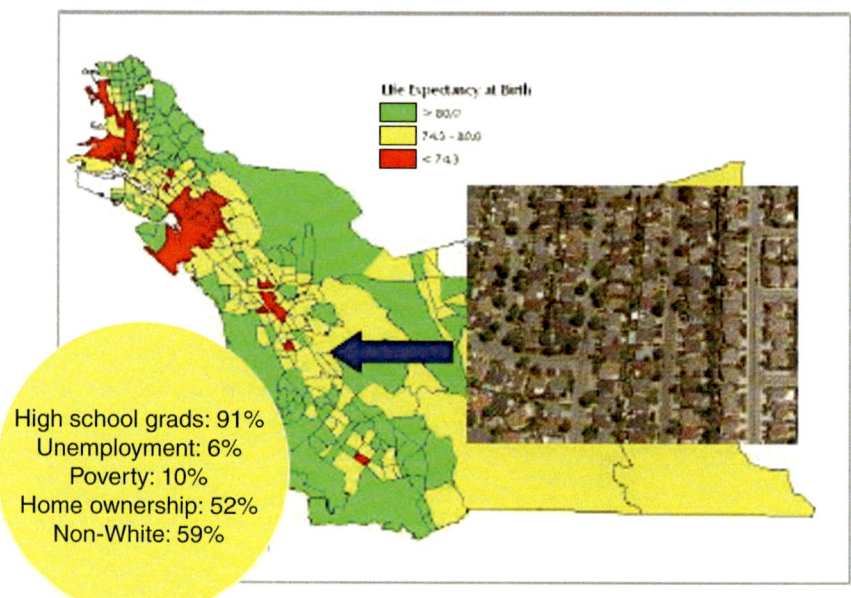

FIGURE 2-3 Neighborhoods in Alameda County with intermediate to long average life expectancy.

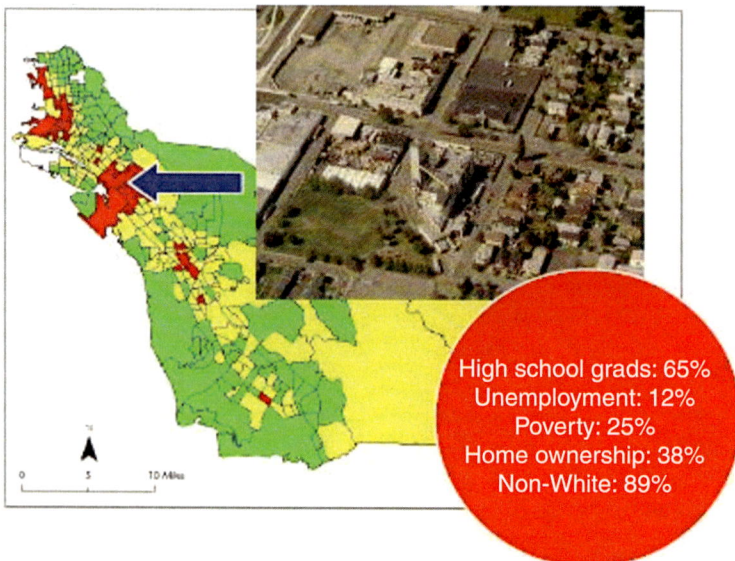

FIGURE 2-4 Neighborhoods in Alameda County with the shortest average life expectancy.

Iton concluded by noting the importance of differentiating "health inequities" and "health disparities." Health inequities are unnecessary, avoidable, and therefore, unjust, whereas health disparities are merely differences in health outcomes divorced from the context in which they are produced. One cannot properly understand health disparities without examining health and social inequity.

THE TWO STEPS BACK FRAMEWORK

Rachel Davis next spoke about the importance of understanding the cumulative impact of living in a stressful environment and its long-term effects on health, particularly for population groups already experiencing inequities. She suggested a model to address the causes of the stressors; strengthen the social, economic, and physical environments of those neighborhoods; and empower those groups most affected by inequities. Investments in communities and efforts to learn to work across government levels and across sectors within a government are needed. In turn, this will lead to a sustainable system for promoting health equity.

Davis's interest in creating and sustaining systems arose from her previous experience as a social worker. She told a story about working in a residential treatment facility for emotionally disturbed children. One day, an underdeveloped 4-year-old boy came to the facility, accompanied by paperwork saying that the boy had "failed" 14 foster placements in the past year. How can a 4-year-old fail in foster placement? In reality, the system is failing him, rather than the other way around.

Davis outlined a set of policy principles to guide efforts to reduce health disparities (see Appendix A). These principles were adapted from the Alameda County Public Health Department report (2008) described earlier by Iton. Related to these policy principles is the Two Steps Back framework (Figure 2-5). The model begins with a consideration of medical care.

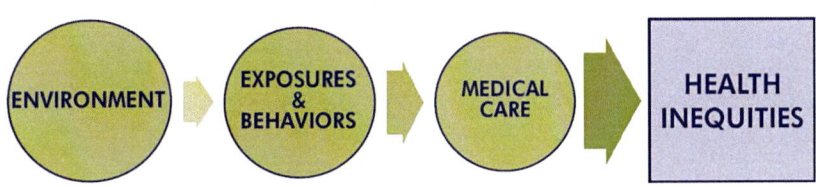

FIGURE 2-5 Two Steps Back framework.

Clearly, access to high-quality and culturally and linguistically appropriate care is critical to improved health outcomes. A wealth of data, including data from the Institute of Medicine (IOM) report *Unequal Treatment: Confronting Racial and Ethnic Disparities in Health Care* (IOM, 2003), document the disparities between people of color and whites in health outcomes that occur because of a lack of access to health care for people of color.

However, taking a step back, access to medical care alone is not enough to eliminate health disparities. Exposures and behaviors also need to be addressed. A wide variety of research indicates a set of nine behaviors and exposures that are linked to major causes of premature death: tobacco, diet and activity patterns, alcohol, microbial agents, toxic agents, firearms, sexual behavior, motor vehicles, and inappropriate drug use. Reducing one's exposure to these behaviors reduces one's risk of injury and illness.

Taking a second step back, the model suggests that exposures and behaviors are shaped by the environment in which a person lives. This offers an opportunity to prevent injuries and illness before their onset by considering the root factors (for example, poverty, racism, and other community factors). A focus on changing exposures and individual behaviors cannot begin until the root causes are addressed and the ways in which they play out in communities are altered. Quoting an earlier IOM report, Davis noted that "it is unreasonable to expect that people will change their behavior easily when so many forces in the social, cultural, and physical environment conspire against such change" (IOM, 2000, p. 4).

Looking more specifically at policy issues linked to negative outcomes in the environment, Davis suggested a number of examples: criminal justice laws, hiring practices, redlining in residential areas, and more recently, the subprime lending fiasco that disproportionately affected low-income communities and people of color.

Violence is another environmental stressor and more often occurs in low-income communities of color. For some young people, violence is a pervasive part of life. The National Center for Post Traumatic Stress estimates that as many as one-third of young people living in the United States are direct victims of violence (U.S. Department of Veterans Affairs, National Center for PTSD, 2011), and that as many as 43 percent of youth experience at least one form of trauma (for example, a school shooting, violence in the community, or physical or sexual abuse). Of those youth who have experienced a traumatic event, between 3 and 15 percent of girls and between 1 and 6 percent of boys will develop posttraumatic stress disorder (U.S. Department of Veterans Affairs, National Center for PTSD, 2011).

Targeted marketing of unhealthy products such as cigarettes and other forms of tobacco, high-alcohol-content malt liquor, and fast food is also a problem in low-income communities. A related problem is a lack of healthy food options, for example, a lack of supermarkets in predominantly African American census tracts.

All of these policy issues shape the environment and have an impact on health. This means that a key means to affect health inequities is providing increased economic and educational opportunity to all, as well as access to health care in low-income communities.

Davis concluded her presentation by speaking about the relationship between health care, health care institutions, and community. The Allina Backyard Project is one such example. A second example is Kaiser Permanente's efforts to start farmers' markets to bring healthy food into low income communities. It is possible, then, to create a system that brings health care, health care institutions, and the community together in support of better health outcomes.

SPECIFIC RECOMMENDATIONS

Larry Cohen, the final presenter and author, described the 32 recommendations from the paper (see Appendix A, page 61, for the complete list), but they can be clustered into four groups. The first is community recommendations. As previously discussed, this means looking at the community environment as a whole, understanding how the root factors that lead to health inequities play out, and emphasizing participation and feeling a sense of ownership and leadership at the community level. An example of this is a housing director who realized that by paying attention to issues like mold and lead paint in the housing stock, she could have an enormous positive impact on health. Similarly, having access to high-quality supermarkets, farmers' markets, walking paths, and safe places to play makes a difference.

The second group consists of health care recommendations (Appendix A, p. 61). These include affordable and accessible health care that is available where people actually live. Technology can also be used to a stronger advantage; for example, cell phones have a 97 percent market penetration in most communities. Cell phones, then, could be used to provide a reminder about a health care appointment or to access health information. Promoting the medical home model is another recommendation.

The third group is systems recommendations (Appendix A, p. 61). These include recommendations such as using community mapping techniques and making health equity a component of every type of new policy, from transportation (providing reliable public transportation and safe places to walk) to housing and agriculture policies.

Cohen offered an example of the efforts of the head librarian in Salinas, California, a major source of the world's lettuce crops. Unfortunately, Salinas also has a very high violent crime rate. In a unique effort to prevent violence among children and youth, the librarian went to every school in

Salinas and gave every child a library card. Library fines were also waived for a year. Three days later, the number of books checked out from the library had tripled. This is a very different way of thinking about health.

The fourth and final group consists of overarching recommendations (Appendix A, p. 61). The nation needs a national strategy, said Cohen, as well as high-level national leadership on health equity issues. Federal resources must support what is happening at the state and local levels, he emphasized.

Cohen concluded his remarks by describing the economics of prevention: According to the Prevention Institute and the Trust for America's Health, with only a $10 annual per capita investment, for every dollar invested in community prevention efforts, by the second year, the community gets that dollar back and a return on investment of an additional dollar. By the fifth year, the return on investment is $5.60 per dollar invested. This provides support to the reasoning that prevention and community wellness efforts should be included in the 2009 federal stimulus package. This implies a very different approach to health and also implies that this is an ideal opportunity to promote health equity as a component of health care reform.

DISCUSSION

Roundtable member Bill Vega asked whether the real goal is to create better living conditions for people living in concentrated poverty neighborhoods. Tony Iton responded that in the United States, many other resources are linked to wealth. In other words, he said, "you can only purchase your way out of harm's way with income in this country." What is needed, then, are policies that decouple wealth from other critical resources, such as health care, dental care, and education.

Iton, who grew up in Canada, noted that Canada provides universal access to health care, universal access to dental care until age 12 years, and subsidized access to education all the way through college. These are policies that decouple wealth from access to critical protective resources. Cohen added that what the paper is really trying to do is promote a different way of thinking about how to pay attention to the community environment to keep people healthy.

Workshop participant Anne Kubisch wondered whether there is scientific support for the unique role of health as the driver of the links between structural issues such as institutional racism and the individual. In particular, the idea of reframing poverty as a public health outcome is a powerful one. In response, Cohen noted that health is a concept that really "hits home" with people. At the same time, the U.S. population does not have a sense that health is an individual right, although this is not the case in Britain, for example, where health is seen to be an individual right. Iton noted the effectiveness of using life expectancy data to look at the injustice of poverty. He believes that using the life expectancy data supports the argument that poverty, educational attainment, and other social determinants affect access to health care and overall health status.

The final question referred to the federal health care reform efforts that got under way in 2009. The participant wondered who will see the savings when the reform is enacted. Cohen noted that a system to track the spending is needed, but that some of the savings will go back to the individual, whereas some of it will go back to the government. This is the thinking behind the Wellness Trust, which is described in several of the pieces of legislation. The funding would come into the trust from a variety of places and would be allocated to a variety of places.

REFERENCES

Alameda County Public Health Department. 2008. *Life and death from unnatural causes: Health and social inequity in Alameda County.* Oakland, CA: Alameda County Public Health Department. http://www.acphd.org/AXBYCZ/Admin/Datareports/00_2008_full_report.pdf (accessed April 28, 2011).

Institute of Medicine. 2000. *Promoting health: Intervention strategies from social and behavioral research.* Washington, DC: National Academy Press.

Institute of Medicine. 2003. *Unequal treatment: Confronting racial and ethnic disparities in healthcare.* Washington, DC: The National Academies Press.

U.S. Department of Veterans Affairs, National Center for PTSD. *PTSD in children and teens.* http://www.ptsd.va.gov/public/pages/ptsd-children-adolescents.asp (accessed May 25, 2011). Washington, DC: U.S. Department of Veterans Affairs, National Center for PTSD.

3

The Phillips-Powderhorn Experience and the Allina Backyard Project

MAYOR R. T. RYBAK

Mayor R. T. Rybak began his comments by acknowledging the efforts of Allina chief executive officer Richard Pettingill. It was his decision, Rybak noted, to move the headquarters of Allina to its current building in a part of Minneapolis experiencing some very deep challenges.

Looking at a map of the city of Minneapolis, Rybak explained that health disparities cluster in certain areas of the city. A look at unemployment rates across the city shows that they cluster in the same places where health disparities do. The same thing occurs with educational disparities. What this means, Rybak said, is that reducing health disparities is really about building holistic communities where a resident is entitled to live in a place where he or she can be fully sustained.

What does this mean from a public policy standpoint? It must first be recognized that any one of these issues cannot be tackled in isolation, but the initial focus needs to be on economic disparities, Rybak said. This includes a focus on housing, access to healthy food, and the ability to access health care when it is needed. Access to job training and job placement are other essential pieces of living a healthy life. Rybak noted that a workforce center is located only about half a block away from Allina headquarters.

Adequate housing is another major component of reducing health disparities. Mayor Rybak developed a housing trust fund that spends $10 million each year on affordable housing efforts. The city also uses the fund to purchase foreclosed homes and place new residents into those homes. The city offers foreclosure prevention sessions as well. He further noted that the foreclosure problem across the United States is a huge human tragedy that requires policy makers to be actively involved in these issues.

Juvenile justice is another focus point in efforts to reduce health disparities. By launching a public health approach to youth violence, the entire community was brought together and a comprehensive approach focusing on prevention was created. This approach involves four key values. First, every young person in Minneapolis is supported by at least one trusted adult in his or her family or community. Second, intervene at the first sign that young people are at risk for violence. The city has stepped up efforts to enforce truancy and curfew laws. A curfew-truancy center where youth are sent also provides family support services; 80 percent of those youth sent to the curfew-truancy center never return. Third, refocus young people who have gone down the wrong path. Lastly, unlearn the culture of violence in the community. The outcome of these programs is that juvenile crime is down 40 percent over the past 2 years in Minneapolis. This is, Rybak said, an example of the importance of focusing on upstream factors.

Referencing the federal health care reform legislation then being discussed in the United States, Rybak observed that it is a "national disgrace" that children and adults in this country lack insurance coverage. At the same time, he said, the population needs to have dramatically different lifestyles. This means a focus on the physical activity aspects of communities. For example, Minneapolis has a bike center and hundreds of miles of bike trails, making the city the number two bicycling city in the United States (Portland, Oregon, is number one). It is essential to create and maintain walkable, sustainable communities.

Another example of making the physical aspects of communities friendlier is the Safe Routes to School initiative. Safe Routes to School is a national initiative that identifies ways in which schools and parent groups can find alternatives to busing to get students to and from school. Designating safe routes on which children may walk to and from school each day and including "human school buses" along the route have the added benefit of helping communities organize. A human school bus consists of parents and other adults who accompany with kids as they walk to school or who stand on their front steps and wave to the children as they walk by. Even a message wishing everyone a good day written in chalk on the sidewalk along where children walk can be a contribution to the human school bus.

The final frontier, Mayor Rybak said, is food: what people are putting in their stomachs. He noted that the local food movement is huge in this country and has led to the launch of a new initiative called Homegrown Minneapolis. This initiative involves creating more community gardens as well as increasing access to high-quality, affordable food in neighborhoods that currently do not have access to such products.

Taking this a step further, Rybak noted his wife's involvement with an effort to better connect children to nature. How can parents and kids be reconnected to the land? How can children be moved from "screen time" to "green time?" By connecting to the land, people become connected to their food and children are able to spend time in natural settings. To summarize, Rybak said, this is really about finding a comprehensive, holistic way to raise a family and thereby find a comprehensive, holistic way to create a community.

DISCUSSION

Following Mayor Rybak's presentation, the audience was invited to ask questions. The first question was from participant Jim Hart of the University of Minnesota, School of Public Health. He asked how the mayor was being supported in his efforts to create holistic communities by the state and federal levels of government.

Rybak responded that, not surprisingly, the support is extraordinarily siloed, in that there is very little discussion across levels of government. For example, although federal and state support for housing is good, the support for youth violence prevention is very episodic. He noted that the current White House has created an urban policy position that is focused on the comprehensive nature of these issues. The mayor also commented on the importance of Michelle Obama planting a garden on the White House grounds.

Workshop participant David Pryor asked whether the city has embraced the mayor's approach to change and whether evidence of lifestyle changes on the part of city residents has been detected. Rybak replied that although all of these initiatives are based in City Hall, they were created in partnership with the community itself. He noted that this is a two-way approach, in that community members must themselves participate in the local food initiative and in exercise. Health care reform cannot be expected to be successful without also focusing on changing individual behaviors, he said.

Sanne Magnan, Commissioner of Health for the state of Minnesota, thanked the mayor for his efforts in helping Minneapolis become one of the pilot communities for a new statewide effort called Steps to a Healthier Minnesota. She explained that she wants to expand this program across the entire state and wondered if lessons learned from the effort could be applied to the future expansion of the program. Rybak responded that the way that communities are built and laid out needs to be rethought. In some cases, this means making access to transit easier; in other cases, this means greater access to different goods within a community. With the population aging, Rybak continued, infrastructure issues must be addressed at the level of Main Street. For example, housing for seniors could be created above a corner grocery store.

Workshop participant Helen Jackson Lockadell asked about strategies to involve the media in better covering the positive things happening in communities. The mayor noted that the media does not always pay attention to the comprehensive nature of these issues. Furthermore, he said that efforts to communicate with people are so much easier now because of new interactive social media such as Facebook and blogging. The need is to stop thinking only about traditional media and start thinking about communicating with people directly, Mayor Rybak commented.

Another workshop participant asked about provisions to use food stamps at farmers' markets. She noted that it is very important for the HIV-positive people who she works with to eat healthy foods. However, it is difficult for them to access healthy foods such as grapes or blueberries because of the restrictions on food stamp usage. Rybak replied that an initiative is under way for farmers' markets to accept payments through electronic benefit transfer. Efforts are also under way to work with grocery store chains to get them to sell more locally grown foods.

When another workshop participant asked the mayor about future efforts to have healthy and sustainable communities, he asked Gretchen Musicant, Commissioner of Health in Minneapolis, to respond. She described the broad network of community clinics in place that provide health care to residents without insurance. She also described a program that is part of the Allina Backyard Project. Portico Healthnet provides people help with connecting to care and to paying for that care. This effort is subsidized by the health care sector, and the hope is to grow this program throughout Minneapolis. However, Rybak noted, the dramatic cuts in health care being proposed at the state level will have a number of consequences for the health department in Minneapolis.

Roundtable chair Nicole Lurie asked the final question. The Allina Backyard Project has reshaped its neighborhood, and similar efforts are under way in North Minneapolis. She wondered what lessons have been learned about the right conditions to make these sorts of changes.

Mayor Rybak replied that good neighborhood capacity, such as local institutional support, is critical. For example, both Allina and Abbott Northwestern Hospital play this role in the Phillips-Powderhorn neighborhood. He also noted the need to be explicit about putting disproportionate help in the areas of the city with disproportionate need. Describing this as "heavy, heavy lifting," Rybak emphasized that extraordinarily broad coalitions must be built and many, many more partners must be involved. The mayor also acknowledged that these efforts are difficult to carry out.

GORDON SPRENGER

Gordon Sprenger is former president and chief executive officer of Allina Health Systems. He presented a historical perspective on efforts that have taken place in the Phillips-Powderhorn neighborhood and began by setting the context. In the mid-1990s, a law that was based on the popularity of health maintenance organizations was implemented in Minnesota. Essentially on the basis of the idea of managing risk, health systems were told that they needed to accept an integrated payment for a population base and manage it. Then, in 1995, 19 hospitals and clinics came together with a major insurance plan into an integrated system that they named "Allina" on the basis of the premise that they could align incentives. The plan was to take a single payment and bring it to an organization like Allina that could then reallocate resources between the provider side and the prevention side. (Although the law was passed, regulations were never approved. Today, most health care deliverers are not part of an integrated system.)

Allina wanted to be an innovator in improving the health of the communities that the organization served. In 1995, these communities were facing many challenges: an aging population, homelessness, suicide, homicides, divorce, stress, households led by single parents, and a changing work environment. All of these challenges led to numerous health and family problems for community residents.

Sprenger described two "ah ha" moments that he experienced at about this time. First, he realized that children were coming to the emergency rooms to be treated for rat bites. No one considered the fact that once the rat bites were treated in the emergency room, the children were going directly back to the same rat-infested homes.

Second, Sprenger described visiting a local park where he spoke to a young mother about whether she had immunized her child. The mother reported that what she was worried about was whether her child would be gunned down in the park, not whether her child was immunized. She was thinking of survival, in other words, and he was thinking about long-term health. This disconnect led to Allina's efforts to solve some of these problems.

Although several corporations and other organizations were operating individual programs within the Phillips-Powderhorn community, no focused cross-agency effort and no comprehensive plan were in place, so a joint business-government-neighborhood partnership was created. The members of the partnership pledged to raise $25 million to improve the community.

Sprenger emphasized here the importance of working in partnership with the other organizations and corporations. He quoted Albert Einstein, saying "The significant problems we face cannot be solved at the same level of thinking we were at when we created them." It was not enough to provide quality health care; what was needed was finding the primary causes of health care problems (violence, smoking, stress) and then finding ways to intervene.

One of the first things the partnership did was to engage in discussions with the police department to find a way in which they could work together to reduce crime and violence in the neighborhood. This effort led to a decrease in violent crimes from 1,227 in 1995 to 467 in 2008. At the same time, housing initiatives were initiated to replace and rehabilitate existing housing on the 14 most blighted blocks.

Other efforts included violence prevention; the creation of protocols to treat victims of abuse; and the establishment of an on-site family service center at a local elementary school that provided health care, social services, and mental health services to children and families. Sprenger offered asthma as an example. Because kids suffering from asthma have high rates of absenteeism, provision of on-site health care services for treatment of asthma resulted in decreased rates of absenteeism and improved school performance.

After realizing that 40 cents of every health care dollar goes to treat a tobacco-related illness, Sprenger decided to take this issue on as well. By contributing lobbying muscle, spending political capital, and working with other health care organizations, those efforts resulted in passage of legislation restricting where one could access tobacco products.

Many observers wondered what all of these efforts had to do with health. Many providers also felt that they were already short on resources to care for their sick patients, let alone to spend their few resources on upstream factors. Sprenger noted, however, that these social problems that the neighborhood residents experienced would become medical problems without some kind of intervention.

Other efforts funded by Allina Systems include

- Creation of the Phillips-Powderhorn Cultural Wellness Center (which will be described in more detail later in this summary).
- Establishment of a free shuttle service for elderly and Medicaid patients to reduce cancellation rates at clinics.
- Paramedic promotion of recreation safety through helmet awareness efforts in the parks to reduce rollerblading injuries.
- Free tattoo removal for former gang members.
- Creation of the Day One Project, a centralized call center with an updated database to help abuse victims find a bed in a shelter, which meant that an abuse victim needing help could locate a vacancy by making one rather than multiple telephone calls.

- Efforts to increase the number of children beginning school with complete immunizations by making shots available throughout the community in the No Shots, No School program, which led to an immunization rate of 98 percent, up from a rate of 60 percent 2 years earlier.
- Establishment of Park House, a day care center for HIV/AIDS patients, where social services as well as health care services are available, which helped prevent hospital emergency room visits.

A major accomplishment was the creation of a health careers partnership. Since 2000, more than 1,200 students have enrolled in the partnership and have graduated and gone on to career-track jobs. The Train to Work program was also created for an important business reason: to provide a future workforce for local hospitals. The program includes work readiness training and has a mentoring component.

Sprenger was chair of the American Hospital Association board at that time, so he had a strong platform from which to describe the program as he traveled throughout the country. He noted that Allina had invested $20 million to get many of the programs described above up and running. Although many were skeptical, Allina believed that their investment in the community was very much a business decision.

RICHARD PETTINGILL

Richard Pettingill is the chief executive officer of Allina. He used the ongoing federal debate over health care reform to frame his comments and began his remarks by stating that the current debate is not about reforming health; rather, it is about reforming how the nation finances health care. The nation's health care system is unaffordable, so a discussion of how to reallocate scarce resources is needed. It is essential, he said, that the dialogue in the debate be changed from one about health *care* to one about what health *is*. He suggested that to see meaningful health care reform, the 32 recommendations from the commissioned paper (Appendix A) need to be discussed and noted that health care reform needs to be seen as health promotion and prevention.

Pettingill related a story about the importance of determining what "health" means to people. Atum Azzahir hosted a community meeting where residents were asked the question, "How do you define health?" Having never been asked this question, after a stunned silence, the responses included "living my life without despair," "I hope my kids have a future," and "I know I am not dead, but I'm not certain I'm alive." These definitions are fundamentally different from those of clinicians.

Pettingill likens the current situation to a perfect storm: health care reform legislation will provide incremental improvements and try to repair a system that is already broken. What is needed instead is investment in the design of an entirely new system.

As an integrated delivery system, Allina has a board of directors that has challenged the organization to, as Pettingill said, "create a revolution in health care." It is not enough to tinker around the edges, the board emphasized. The organization should be "at the forefront of that revolution."

Although acute and episodic care will always be an important part of the Allina system, now the emphasis is more on going upstream to focus on wellness, prevention, and chronic disease management. An electronic information system is also an important component of the organization so that the care received can be measured.

One example of how such an electronic information system can be used can be seen in a project launched by Allina in New Ulm, Minnesota, a community of 17,000 residents. The goal is to eliminate heart attacks in 10 years. A community cardiac risk assessment is under way for 10,000 of those residents. Then, moving upstream, residents at risk of cardiac arrest will be placed in a model of care that includes prevention, wellness, and chronic disease management. This is a change in how models of providing care get rewarded because prior to this, Allina would have been paid only for providing care to a heart attack patient in the emergency room. Scarce resources need to be reallocated to focus on social circumstances and behavioral issues (Figure 3-1). Rather than investing resources solely on health care access, investments in improving the determinants of health status are needed.

Pettingill also raised the question of what it means to be a not-for-profit organization with a tax exemption. He described a meeting of community leaders where charity health care was discussed, noting that Allina provides free care in the community worth $135 million. Pettingill noted that the business community suggested that it, the business community, should be the one claiming that benefit, because Allina builds the free care into its rate structure system that then gets passed to the private sector.

This discussion led to the formation in 2008 of Allina's Center for Healthcare Innovation. Encompassing three projects—the Heart of New Ulm, the Backyard Initiative, and the Allina Patient Safety Center—the center's purpose is to advance initiatives that improve overall health and well-being in the communities that Allina serves. These initiatives, in turn, will lead to the creation of national models that can be replicated locally. Allina is investing $100 million over a 5-year period in the Center for Healthcare Innovation. The center will also include a research component, in conjunction with the University of Minnesota's School of Public Health.

Pettingill described the neighborhood where the Backyard Initiative

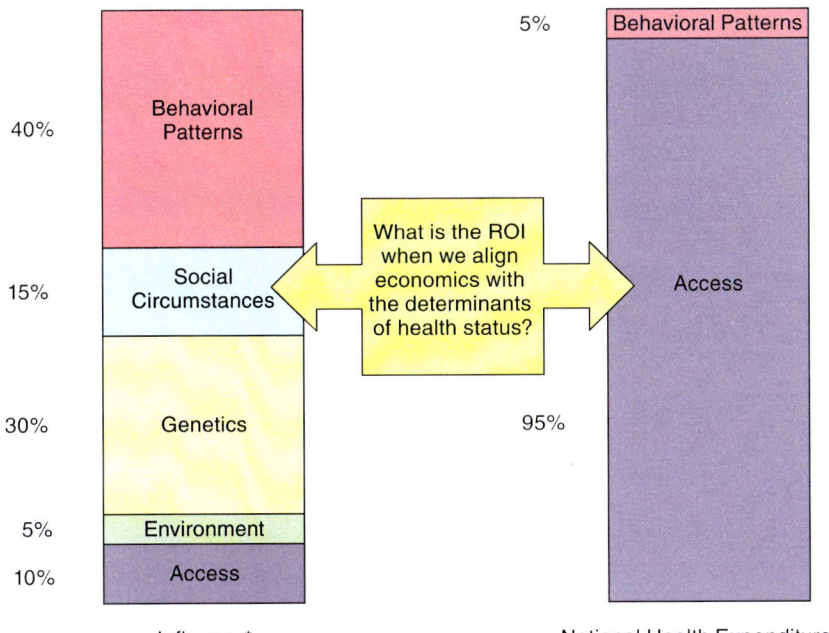

FIGURE 3-1 Aligning expenditures with determinants of health (* = McGinnis et al., 2002; ** = Brown et al., 1992).

is based. The neighborhood has a population of 45,000 people and high rates of unemployment, poverty, and subprime mortgages. At the same time, 50 not-for-profit organizations are present in the neighborhood, so resources are available. The real challenge is to get these organizations to collaborate, not compete, and to direct the limited resources in the same direction. The Backyard Initiative also has a strong Residents Council and buy-in from community businesses. The police department and the city public health department are both partners with the community as well. The role of Allina is to be a convener of people and to be a collaborator with the organizations.

The Backyard Initiative has a strong focus on prevention. For example, a childhood visual acuity screening was held in the neighborhood. Seven hundred children were screened, and 20 percent of those children needed—but did not have—corrective lenses. Clearly, this will affect the academic achievement of that 20 percent. Similarly, it is estimated that 50 percent of the children in the neighborhood have never had a dental exam. This, too, will affect learning, Pettingill explained.

Another partner of the Backyard Initiative is the Minnesota Early

Learning Foundation. A new project, the Early Learning Initiative, is being launched. Its goal is to encourage literacy in prekindergarten children. This, in turn, will affect graduation rates, incarceration rates, and health status. A health risk assessment effort is also linked to the Early Learning Initiative so that preschoolers who need visual and dental care can access it early in life.

Still needed in the neighborhood, Pettingill said, is a medical home as well as a social home. This will involve further partnering to ensure access for residents to the medical care delivery system, the public health system, the educational system, the social system, the social services system, and the economic system.

SANNE MAGNAN

Sanne Magnan is the Commissioner of Health in Minnesota. Her presentation focused on (1) health care reform efforts in Minnesota and how those efforts have affected health disparities; (2) efforts and priorities at the state level to reduce health disparities via Minnesota's Eliminating Health Disparities Initiative (EHDI), launched in 2001; and (3) working with policy makers to reduce health disparities.

Health Care Reform Efforts

Sanne Magnan began her comments by describing the strengths of the state of health care in Minnesota. She noted that the health plans in the state (e.g., Medica, Blue Cross and Blue Shield of Minnesota, HealthPartners, and UCare) are required by law to be nonprofit. The state also has many integrated health care organizations, as well as a strong community clinic system and safety net system. In relation to the situations in other states, Minnesota has some of the highest-quality health care and some of the lowest health care costs in the nation, Magnan said. At the same time, every dollar that goes toward health care costs takes dollars away from other determinants of health, such as prevention, healthy behaviors, education, and affordable housing.

Minnesota's health care reform law, passed in 2008, begins with an investment in public health and prevention through a statewide health improvement program. Initially called the Statewide Health Promotion Program, it built upon the Centers for Disease Control and Prevention's (CDC's) Steps to a Healthier U.S. model. State legislators, however, wanted to focus on health improvement rather than promotion, so the name was changed to the Statewide Health Improvement Program (SHIP). SHIP aims to help reduce the burden of chronic disease by focusing on the two leading preventable causes of illness and death: tobacco use and obesity. Through a competitive grant process, funding for SHIP was awarded to local public health agencies (community health boards) and tribal governments. SHIP now covers all 87 counties in Minnesota and all tribal regions whose governments accept state funding.

SHIP focuses on making upstream changes to policies, systems, and environments to reduce tobacco use and exposure and to increase physical activity and good nutrition. Making those upstream changes is critical, Magnan said. Although improving the health care system is a worthy goal, if the only thing that happens is that more people enter the health care system to receive treatment, nothing is really solved. Upstream investments like those made by SHIP can help prevent disease before it starts.

Other components of Minnesota's health care reform efforts include improving transparency about the quality and cost of health care, the creation of a quality incentive program for providers, and the implementation across the state of medical homes, which link the primary health care system with resources available in the community. Another activity supported at the state level by the health department is implementation of health information technology. By implementing electronic health records, Magnan noted, it will be easier to collect race and ethnicity data. Currently, more focused approaches are needed to collect such data, and those data are desperately needed to inform the activities needed to address disparities. By legislative mandate, both SHIP and health care homes will be evaluated by how well disparities are decreased.

Eliminating Health Disparities Initiative Efforts and Priorities in Minnesota

One critical aspect of Minnesota's EHDI is to invest in building leadership capacity within communities of color and Native American populations. The initial approach focused on the eight key areas listed in Box 3-1.

At the same time, the health department is making a conscious effort to move toward a focus on upstream factors and the social determinants of health. This upstream approach—rather than a focus only on the health care system—should assist with reducing multiple health disparities. Moving the focus upstream can maximize the funding available to reduce health disparities by reaching more people because by focusing only on the provision of services to individuals, only a limited number of individuals can be reached. For example, Minnesota has approximately 750,000 residents who are people of color or American Indians, yet the existing funding can reach only 55,000 individuals with direct services. Working upstream in policy, systems, and environmental changes to address healthy behaviors, education, job development, the environment, etc., will allow a greater impact on more people in the state. Minnesota's Freedom to Breathe act is an example of an upstream policy initiative that begins to reduce health

> **BOX 3-1**
> **Eliminating Health Disparities Initiative (EHDI)**
>
> Statewide effort to eliminate disparities in 8 areas:
>
> | | |
> |---|---|
> | Infant Mortality | Diabetes |
> | Childhood/Adult Immunization | HIV/AIDS and STIs |
> | Cardiovascular Disease | Breast/Cervical Cancer |
> | Violence/Unintentional Injury | Healthy Youth Development |

disparities. By mandating clean indoor air for all restaurants, bars, and institutions, workers and patrons are protected from secondhand smoke. This is true for people of any race, ethnicity, or socioeconomic status.

Other particular initiatives are essential to reducing health disparities. For example, in addition to the areas listed in Box 3-1, reducing tuberculosis is listed as a priority in the EHDI legislation. Magnan also noted the importance of building social capital and enhancing social interconnections as a strategy to eliminate health disparities. One example of this can be seen in state efforts to improve emergency preparedness. These efforts led to meetings between public health officials and other community officials, such as chiefs of fire departments and chairs of school boards. These connections across organizations can assist in tackling a myriad of problems. The establishment and use of medical care homes are another way to increase social capital, link people with cultural resources, and enhance work to eliminate health disparities.

Working with Policy Makers

Sanne Magnan noted the importance of using language that policy makers (e.g., legislators) understand. For example, rather than talking about physical inactivity and unhealthy eating, which is what she called "public health speak," talk instead about "obesity." Discussing the increasing rates of obesity among U.S. children—the children people see on the streets and playgrounds in their communities every day—is much more compelling than describing the problem only in public health terms. The creation of community gardens with the involvement of families and children is another example of a compelling story for legislators.

Another important lesson learned about working with legislators is to focus on solutions that can solve multiple problems. For example, Minnesota is discussing using some of the same infrastructure for both SHIP and emergency preparedness programs. Treating obesity as a disaster event or incident, like any other emergency, is an approach that could address many problems, Magnan explained. In addition, an infrastructure like that used for SHIP that focuses on policies, systems, and environmental interventions could be used to tackle other issues, such as alcohol abuse.

Finally, Magnan indicated that the use of economic data is also helpful when working with the legislature. She used the example of sharing with the legislature the economic consequences of tobacco use and obesity, explaining that unless these two health care issues are addressed, the annual cost of health care for the state could be as much as $3.4 billion.

DISCUSSION AND QUESTIONS

All of the morning speakers (Cohen, Iton, Rybak, Sprenger, Pettingill, and Magnan) responded to questions. Jeff Levi asked the first question, which referenced the health care reform efforts going on at the federal level. He asked how the federal government could best support the positive efforts under way in Minnesota. He followed up by asking Magnan to address the role of prevention in Minnesota's health programs.

Sanne Magnan responded by referring first to the American Recovery and Reinvestment Act, passed by the U.S. Congress in early 2009. That legislation included approximately $650 million for community-level health and wellness programs. She noted the importance of ensuring that those funds get to the local level for use in programs like the Steps to a Healthier U.S. program currently funded by the CDC.

Sanne Magnan also described the perception that the federal efforts in health care reform address only access to care and not the overuse and inefficiencies in the health care system. The National Priorities Partnership is one organization trying to bring to bear a framework that focuses on the problem of overuse. Palliative care and safety issues must also be addressed.

Reforming Medicare payment models is another piece of the federal effort that Magnan believes needs to be addressed. States like Minnesota, she said, are actually disadvantaged because of the way that Medicare pays providers.

Richard Pettingill suggested that the public health community needs to show some outrage to become actively involved in the health care debate. He noted that the book *Freakonomics*, in describing how people ascertain risks, describes a trade-off between hazards and outrage that must be balanced. The number of people who die each year of heart disease, for example, is an example of a risk with a high hazard but low levels of outrage. High levels of outrage (and a low level of hazards), on the other hand, occurs when a child dies because of a gunshot wound. What is needed, Pettingill said, is greater levels of outrage on the part of the public health community. This outrage needs to be brought to the federal health care reform debate.

A representative from the Minneapolis Urban League asked the panel about the problem of the very small amount of resources available to communities of color. For example, she said, many children in Minneapolis eat hot Cheetos or other junk foods for breakfast. Is there a way, she wondered, to provide incentives to communities to encourage healthier eating? Will SHIP have a role in providing communities of color with incentives for living a healthier lifestyle? Magnan responded that one of the strengths of SHIP is that local communities will have a menu of interventions from which to choose.

A participant from the Association for Nonsmokers described her experience attending the state's SHIP conference. She noted that some members of the audience see health care reform efforts to be a move toward socialism. Additionally, some participants at the conference expressed negative feelings about using taxpayer dollars to try to change individual behavior. In fact, some participants at the conference believed that attempting to change this behavior is not an appropriate role for government at all.

Magnan replied that this is an example of "democracy in action." Consideration of community health requires both individual responsibility and community responsibility. For example, if a person wants to go walking outdoors, it is his or her responsibility to put on shoes and go out the front door. At the same time, however, if the community has no sidewalks, no streetlights, or high levels of crime, the responsibility becomes that of the community. Rather than seeing this as socialism, Magnan commented, this is just good public policy.

Joel Weissman, an afternoon speaker, offered his own examples of the critical link between individual responsibility and community responsibility. People will not go out walking, he said, unless the community makes it possible to go out walking. Weissman noted that many elderly people move to Florida because in their home states snow does not get shoveled from the sidewalks and they end up feeling trapped in their homes. It is possible, he said, to combine a focus on individual behavior with public policy.

Weissman is a backyard gardener, growing cherry tomatoes, blueberries, and raspberries, and discovered that his children and their friends were snacking from the garden. At the same time, he noted, they still like pizza and Cheetos as much as ever. So, only so much can be done to encourage individual responsibility without ensuring that opportunities exist as well. A person cannot eat healthy food without access to gardens, farmers' markets, or good grocery stores.

Sarah Greenfield, a community organizer with Take Action Minnesota and Make Health Happen, asked about access to high-quality, affordable health care. Commenting that this was only one recommendation out of 32 in the commissioned paper by Larry Cohen, Anthony Iton, Rachel Davis, and Sharon Rodriguez, she asked if the changes that occur nationally or in the state because of health care reform would affect the public delivery of health care to the poor, the elderly, and other groups with limited resources.

Anthony Iton responded that it is imperative to consider health care an important social good. The goal is to align the incentives so that people understand that their own personal interests are inextricably tied to the health issues of others in their community. He noted that the current health care reform debate is really about payment reform rather than health care reform and that this is a frightening distraction from the real issues. It is essential, Iton said, to ensure that community-based prevention efforts are at the core of health care reform.

Larry Cohen noted that not everyone shares the perspective that prevention should be the centerpiece of health care reform. Other advocates feel that the emphasis on prevention is a distraction. Clearly, he said, one is not going to work without the other; the two groups of advocates must learn to work together.

Richard Pettingill, in response to Sarah Greenfield's question, commented that it is essential to bring the mainstream health care delivery system into the debate as a collaborator with communities and public health officials. Rather than seeing the current efforts as either health reform or health care reform, it should be a dialogue that includes both health reform and health care reform.

Sam Nussbaum asked Sanne Magnan about the role of reducing waste and inefficiency in the health care system. He proposed that Minnesota could be a model for other states looking to reduce the cost of care, and asked Magnan to talk about efforts within the state to get costs under control.

In response, Magnan stated that Minnesota's health reform efforts have three goals: first, to improve population health; second, to improve the health care experience for the consumer; and third, to improve affordability. As an example, she described the state's efforts to create a system for high-tech diagnostic imaging (magnetic resonance imaging and computed tomography scans) across communities and health plans. Any patient who is given a high-tech diagnostic imaging test should have this information embedded in that patient's electronic medical records. In this way, a system has been put into place to ensure that this valuable but expensive resource is being used wisely across communities.

Richard Pettingill offered a second response to Nussbaum's question. Although Minnesota is ranked at the top of all states in terms of health status and educational achievement, it is also true that the state has a high tax rate. In comparison, Georgia has a very low tax rate but among the worst high school graduation rates in the country. Also, Medicare reimbursement rates are higher in Georgia than in Minnesota. At the same time, the quality of health care is lower in Georgia than in Minnesota.

Nicole Lurie noted that the federal stimulus funding contains investments in areas that directly affect health outcomes, such as early childhood education and housing. Her perspective is that these should be considered important health investments.

Joel Weissman asked about the role of evaluation in establishing medical homes. Magnan explained that they relied upon a very participatory process that first involved setting up criteria and outcomes. She noted that it is essential to look at outcomes because of the need to be held accountable for better health and improved affordability.

Roundtable chair Nicole Lurie asked the final question, which was whether health care organizations such as health insurers and hospital systems should be allowed to have nonprofit status. She explained that there is a national movement among public health leaders to request evidence for the community benefits that a health care organization provides in order to determine that it is providing an adequate amount of community care. Thus, the organization must provide concrete evidence in order to maintain its nonprofit status.

Gordon Sprenger said that his view is that the difference between for-profit and nonprofit systems is what the organization does with the profits. In a for-profit organization, those profits go back to the shareholders; in a nonprofit organization, those profits should be invested back into the organization itself and into the community that it serves. He noted the importance of national leadership on the question of how resources are allocated and said that this is at the core of health care reform.

Sprenger also mentioned the role of philanthropic organizations. Explaining that philanthropies have few constraints on how funding is allocated, he said that as health care reform continues to be evaluated, the private foundation environment also needs to be examined.

Mike Christensen, a member of Mayor Rybak's staff, also responded by saying that public health leadership needs to adopt a new "fundamentalism" about reducing health disparities in Minnesota. He noted that of the health disparities that Sanne Magnan described in her presentation, many involve sex or violence behaviors. These behaviors, in turn, can lead to despair, hopelessness, and a lack of future orientation. Low-income urban populations need more than a new brochure, Christensen said; they need career ladders and affordable housing. Society needs to "get real about the interventions," he commented. He also explained that Allina had tripled the amount of hiring that it does from the surrounding neighborhoods, and that Wells Fargo Mortgage had invested $35 million in housing in the surrounding area. In conclusion, Christensen said, these are the kinds of interventions that need to happen.

REFERENCES

Brown, R., J. Corea, B. Luce, A. Elixhauser, and S. Sheingold. 1992. Effectiveness in disease and injury prevention estimated national spending on prevention—United States, 1988. *Morbidity and Mortality Weekly Report* 41(29):529–531.

McGinnis, J. M., P. Williams-Russo, and J. R Knickman. 2002. The case for more active policy attention to health promotion. *Health Affairs* 21(2):78–93.

4

Health Disparities in Great Britain and Massachusetts: Policy Solutions

Roundtable cochair Mildred Thompson introduced the session on policy solutions for health disparities in England and Massachusetts by noting that it is important that the investigation of policy solutions not be limited to reducing disparities by ignoring models that are working internationally. She emphasized that this provides the opportunity to hear about the lessons learned in different types of systems. This chapter shares information about disparities reduction efforts in England (Annette Williamson) and the state of Massachusetts (Joel Weissman). Tom Granatir provided some introductory material about the health care system in England. The United Kingdom of Great Britain and Northern Ireland (the United Kingdom) is made up of four separate countries (Wales, Scotland, England, and Ireland), and each country has its own National Health Service (NHS).

THE HEALTH CARE SYSTEM IN ENGLAND

The NHS in England is the fourth largest employer in the world, after the Chinese army, the Indian railroads, and Wal-Mart. Geographically, the entire United Kingdom (all four countries) is about the size of Oregon, with a population of just under 61 million people. The population of England alone is slightly above 50 million people. The population is also quite diverse; the NHS website is translated into 12 different languages, and 5 of them are languages from the Indian subcontinent.

The NHS was founded to meet the needs of the British people as England was coming out of World War II. Lord Beveridge, an economist who was one of the primary forces behind the creation of the NHS in 1948,

> **BOX 4-1**
> **Beveridge—The Five Giants**
>
> - Want — or the need for an adequate income for all
> - Disease — or the need for access to health care
> - Ignorance — or the need for access to educational opportunity
> - Squalor — or the need for adequate housing
> - Idleness — or the need for gainful employment

described these needs as being not only health but also "want, ignorance, squalor, disease, and idleness" (Box 4-1) (Beveridge, 1942). The belief was that all of these needs had to be addressed to make any progress on any one of these needs. All hospitals and health care providers (except physicians, who remained independent) were nationalized to standardize the system.

The NHS is funded through general taxation, and care is provided free at the point of care. Every citizen is expected to register with a general practitioner. Although some treatment options are not covered because of coverage decisions by NHS's standard-setting body, primary care is free.

Until 1997, the NHS was essentially a monopoly of care provision. Long waiting lists for services came as a result of very low funding levels for the NHS. In 1997, the Labor Party moved to modernize the system and reduce the waiting times. The new system was more patient centered and gave people more choices, but also reduced waiting times. This was what NHS termed "joined-up care," which also included efforts to integrate services for people living with chronic health conditions.

The new system also moved control and responsibility for health outcomes from the national level to the local level. The NHS is organized into 10 different regions called "strategic health authorities." These authorities, in turn, provide oversight to 152 primary care trusts. Each trust is responsible for health assessments and for organizing all of the health care services needed for the population in its catchment area. Each primary care trust, then, represents a local health economy of between 400,000 and 500,000 residents. Primary care trusts are thus similar to geography-based health plans in the United States. Unlike U.S. health plans, however, the trusts engage in population-based health planning (see Figure 4-1 for the NHS model).

Despite the reorganization, the system still has large health inequalities. In light of these inequalities, one of the top five reform goals of the reorganized NHS is the reduction of health inequalities, and the government is working to establish specific targets to reduce these inequalities. This is a

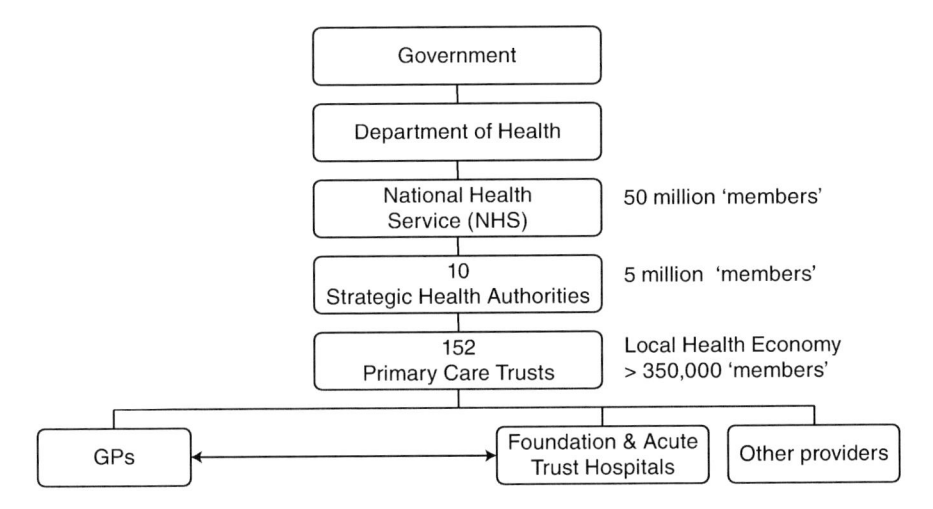

HEALTH DISPARITIES IN GREAT BRITAIN AND MASSACHUSETTS

FIGURE 4-1 Organization of the NHS.

critical difference from the U.S. health system, as the United States has no way to link national goal-setting efforts with mandated actions. The NHS, in contrast, has the ability to set explicit goals and then implement efforts to meet those goals.

The target-setting process, however, has been a source of debate in England. One of the ongoing arguments is whether targets should be set nationally or devolved to the local level. This reveals another cultural difference of the system in England from the U.S. system: in the United States, much of government is already devolved to the state level.

Unlike the United States, England has a wide understanding and acceptance of the principle that health inequalities are based on social determinants. Focusing on social determinants requires working across institutional boundaries. This idea, too, is widely accepted in England.

Another component of the English health care system are the National Support Teams (NSTs), created in 2006. NSTs provide technical support to the local primary care trusts. They have targeted the key drivers of health inequalities in infant mortality, for example, and have created interventions that are potential solutions.

One example of a health inequality that can be addressed by interventions is smoking rates. Some areas in England have smoking rates above 70 percent. Use of a mix of primary and secondary prevention in those areas can affect life expectancy gaps and treat chronic diseases, such as cardiovascular disease. This is especially true if interventions target people at fairly young ages.

> **BOX 4-2**
> **Spearhead Areas**
>
> - Local Authorities in bottom fifth for 3 or more of the following:
>   —Male life expectancy at birth
>   —Female life expectancy at birth
>   —Cancer mortality rate
>   —Cardiovascular disease mortality rate
>   —Index of Multiple Deprivation 2004 (Local Authority Summary), average score
>
> - The Spearhead Group comprises 70 Local Authority areas mapping to 62 Primary Care Trusts

Those geographic areas with "high deprivation" (an area that has significantly worse health outcomes and/or high rates of poverty and social deprivation, such as the areas with high smoking rates described above) are called "spearheads." Seventy local areas of high deprivation that cross 62 of the primary care trusts are spearheads (Box 4-2). These spearheads are given more resources to address health inequalities because the people in those areas have greater needs.

In short, England has the ability to set explicit health goals for its populace. The national government then gives decision-making power and technical assistance to local health authorities to meet those goals. This model is very different from that in the United States.

Granatir also discussed the use of electronic health records in the United States and England. For example, he said, although the degree of adoption of electronic records in United States is high, little interoperability or integration exists across sites. Therefore, the United States has little ability to capture and track patients across systems. England, he said, is better at blending social and commercial data (such as purchasing patterns that are tracked by Mosaic) with health data to build more specific, relevant health interventions.

NATIONAL SUPPORT TEAMS: EMERGING THEMES FROM THE INFANT MORTALITY SUPPORT TEAM VISITS

Annette Williamson is the program manager of the Department of Health National Support Team for infant mortality in England. She is a trained registered nurse, midwife, and health visitor and has worked as both an operational manager and, more recently, as a commissioner of

Children and Young People Services. She has worked within the NHS for 30 years, predominantly in Birmingham, the second largest city in the United Kingdom.

NSTs are designed to provide assistance through consultancy-style site visits to those areas experiencing the highest rates of infant mortality. A multiagency team of experts reviews the health and social care provided in a locale to provide the locale with specific, tailor-made recommendations. The team includes members of the NHS, the local government, and other sectors such as voluntary and not for profit organizations. The process is designed to be a supportive experience for the locale (see Box 4-3 for more information).

NSTs use a triangulated approach to assess demographics, health status, and access to social care (Figure 4-2). NSTs review a spectrum of areas during their visits, including housing, maternal and infant nutrition, immunizations, screenings, and rates of tobacco use and teen pregnancy.

The NST model is based on a 4-day visit to the primary care trust. At the end of the fourth day, the chief executive of the trust is provided with a comprehensive package of feedback that includes key recommendations. A series of follow-up visits by the NST also occurs. The feedback from those primary care trusts that the NST has visited has been very positive, with the trusts reporting that they value the support and recommendations that the NST gives to address challenging health inequalities.

All recommendations are evidence based and include the identification of good practices during the visit. The NST places emphasis on creating practical solutions and assisting the local team members with thinking

---

BOX 4-3
What Are National Support Teams?

National Support Teams (NSTs) provide consultancy-style, expert and peer tailored delivery support to health partnerships in England—Primary Care Trusts (PCTs), NHS Trusts, and Local Authorities.

Areas offered support are identified principally on performance and who would most benefit. Discussions take place with Government Offices and Strategic Health Authorities prior to offer being made to individual areas. Local areas are the clients.

Expertise drawn from the NHS, Local Government and Third Sector (voluntary and not for profit organizations) with expertise in relevant topic areas, change management, commissioning and public health. Matching expertise principle used.

NST model

Population Health and Well-being

Systematic enquiry with questions for key stakeholders

Systematic and scaled interventions by frontline services

Fitness for Purpose
Re: Health and Well-being
Leadership
Partnership
Organisational Arrangements
Vision, Strategy and Commissioning
Data and Needs Assessment
Communications, Social Marketing and Community Engagement
Workforce Capacity and Training

Systematic community engagement

Personal Health and Well-being

Frontline service engagement with the community in different settings

Community Health and Well-being

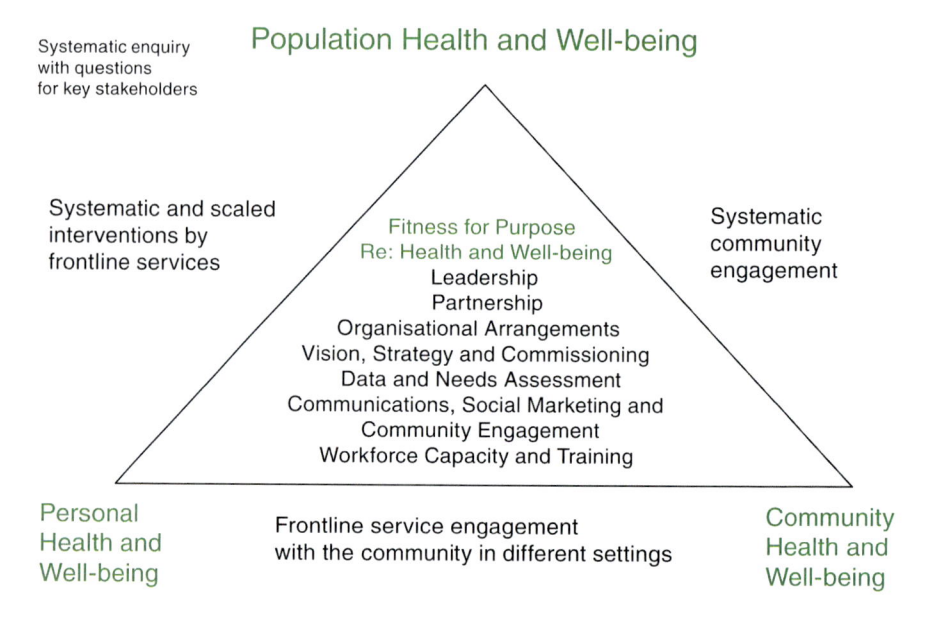

FIGURE 4-2 NST model.

through their priorities. The team also addresses means of reducing health inequalities and improving standards of care and health outcomes. Since their inception in 2006, the NSTs have made more than 200 visits to local health trusts and spearhead areas.

The infant mortality NST has an ambitious goal of reducing the infant mortality rate for the population with routine and manual occupations (which the United Kingdom Office for National Statistics defines as individuals with lower supervisory and technical occupations or semiroutine and routine occupations). At the end of 2010, that population had a 10 percent higher infant mortality rate than the general population. Nevertheless, according to Williamson, the data demonstrate that significant inroads to meeting this target are being made.

Overall, the NHS works to ensure that all resources are targeted to those with the greatest health need. The NHS reviews its investments in these areas via contracts, health impact assessments, and equity audits. For example, reducing teen pregnancy rates would yield reductions in sudden infant deaths, as the infants of teenage mothers have an increased risk of mortality. Thus, the infant mortality team takes specific interest in teenage mothers and single mothers. Ethnicity and homelessness are also considered to be critical factors affecting infant mortality. Williamson outlined five emerging strategic themes from her work with the infant mortality NST. These are outlined in Box 4-4.

> **BOX 4-4**
> **Emerging Strategic Themes from Implementation Plan for Reducing Health Inequalities in Infant Mortality**
>
> Knowing the target, knowing your gap
> Make the target part of everyday business
> Taking responsibility and engaging communities
> Matching resources to need
> Focusing on what can be done

Maternal obesity has an impact on infant mortality rates as well (obesity is considered a major health problem in England). Other areas of focus include reducing child poverty rates and reducing smoking rates. Reducing overcrowding is also seen as critical because children living under overcrowded conditions are 10 times more likely to catch meningitis and 3 times more likely to develop chronic respiratory conditions. Rates of sudden infant death syndrome also increase in overcrowded environments.

Williamson outlined some emerging themes from the work of the infant mortality NST. First, she said, the target must be clear and must incorporate relevant social factors as well as health needs. In other words, a holistic approach with an overarching set of strategies is required. She noted that, in particular, housing and social care services alongside voluntary organizations have clear roles to play. Health care, social care, and voluntary organizations prepare local area agreements, which are cross-cutting plans that incorporate service delivery, and must agree to the targets and to deliver services together to affect the target. Second, social marketing is a key component in focusing the local community on meeting health targets. Regional social marketing advisors within each strategic health authority help increase community awareness and engagement. The use of social marketing strategies is growing throughout England. Such strategies include the use of tools such as Mosaic to give providers an understanding of different populations and their preferences and needs.

Innovative ways to deliver information and services are also developing. For example, call centers are being used more widely, and service delivery is occurring at nontraditional venues, such as faith centers and schools. Text messaging is also being used to contact residents. Williamson highlighted that the NHS has an infinite demand for services and finite resources; therefore, services need to be commissioned to ensure that they have an impact on those populations at the greatest risk.

The role of data cannot be underestimated, and the NHS is developing a major information technology (IT) program that will herald an electronic health care record system. The current NHS data system is disparate, as local data sources do not always connect. It is hoped that the new IT program will create this connectivity.

Strategic partnerships are another component of the NHS. For example, health and well-being partnerships include housing departments to prioritize health and well-being priorities for local authorities. These partnerships have been developed across every local health authority within England.

Williamson concluded by outlining next steps for the infant mortality NST. Team staff members are developing a workshop based on strategies to deal with child poverty, and development of a database of "best practices" is under way. Site visits to local areas will continue to provide support in reaching and maintaining goals.

DISCUSSION

Roundtable member Tom Granatir noted that the Centers for Disease Control and Prevention do conduct social marketing campaigns in the United States. For example, public service announcements target smoking cessation. He noted that, in fact, the idea for using commercial marketing techniques to achieve social goals actually originated in the United States.

An audience member asked about the "rigid, hierarchical class system" in England and whether that affects infant mortality rates in disadvantaged populations. Annette Williamson responded that they consider quintiles of deprivation in a given population. A deeper look at the bottom quintile is then chosen to detect the factors contributing to life in the bottom quintile such as poverty, access to transportation, and so on. Age and ethnicity are also considered. Interventions are then targeted to the bottom two quintiles.

HEALTH DISPARITY-RELATED ACTIVITIES UNDER MASSACHUSETTS HEALTH CARE REFORM

Joel Weissman is the senior health policy advisor to the secretary within the Massachusetts Executive Office of Health and Human Services. His presentation focused on health disparity-related activities as a part of the health care reform law in Massachusetts, referred to as Chapter 58.

Chapter 58: Massachusetts Health Care Reform

Weissman provided an overview of Chapter 58 to lay the groundwork for the discussion of health disparities. The principle behind the law is to make coverage a shared responsibility between individuals (an individual mandate), employers ("play or pay"), and the state government (Medicaid expansions). In 2008, after passage of the law, only 2.6 percent of the population in the state was uninsured. This is by far the lowest uninsurance rate in the country.

One of the major arguments against the health care reform bill was that costs would go up. Weissman noted that, in fact, health care costs did go up in Massachusetts. However, costs also increased in the rest of the country. In Massachusetts, costs went up proportionally for individuals, employers, and the government, indicating that the coverage mandates did not adversely affect any one group. Public support for the law has been high, with 67 percent supporting the bill in 2007, the year that it passed.

Will Universal Coverage Lead to Reductions in Disparities?

Weissman described a study by Michael McWilliams and colleagues looking at the effects of near-universal Medicare coverage on cardiovascular disease and diabetes rates using NHANES (National Health and Nutrition Examination Survey) data. They found that, "with near-universal Medicare coverage after age 65 years, differences in systolic blood pressure, hemoglobin A1c levels, or total cholesterol levels reduced substantially" (McWilliams et al., 2009, p. 510). He also noted a press release by the Commonwealth Fund stating that universal coverage could be a possible means of reducing these types of disparities in the general population. The question is, would near-universal coverage in Massachusetts lead to similar reductions in health disparities?

The first challenge is to look more closely at that 2.6 percent of the population that remains uninsured. The data show that in 2007, Hispanics had the highest levels of uninsurance, at 10.2 percent of the population. By 2009, this rate had declined to 7.2 percent. However, the decline for non-Hispanic whites was from 4.6 percent down to 2.2 percent. In other words, Hispanics still have a higher rate of uninsurance than whites.

Weissman presented data indicating that despite the near-universal coverage in Massachusetts, disparities in access to services as well as in premature or excessive mortality rates for cancer, HIV infection, diabetes, and asthma still exist between racial and ethnic groups. Blacks and Hispanics also have higher rates of hospitalization for many conditions and diseases.

Another way to look at the effects of near-universal coverage is to look at differences in emergency room (ER) visits. Figure 4-3 shows that Hispanics are far more likely to have had an ER visit for a nonemergency health issue than individuals in other racial or ethnicity groups. Similarly, blacks and Hispanics are more likely than whites to report having problems paying medical bills in the past year.

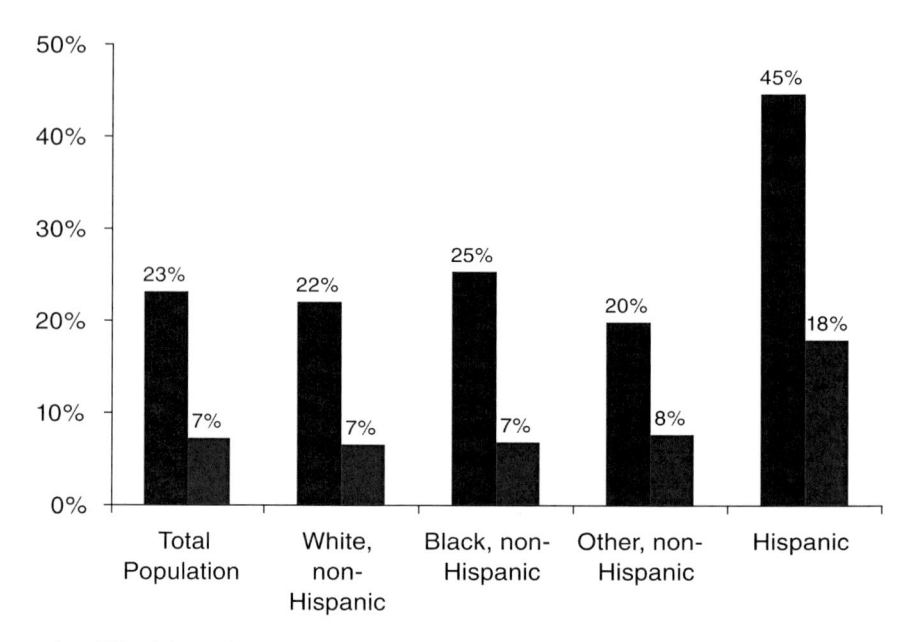

```
50% ─┐
                                                              45%
40% ─

30% ─
                              25%
     23%    22%
20% ─                                    20%
                                                                   18%

10% ─ 7%     7%      7%       8%

 0% ─┴──────┴───────┴────────┴─────────┴─────
    Total   White,  Black,   Other,   Hispanic
  Population non-   non-     non-
            Hispanic Hispanic Hispanic
```

■ Any ER visit   ■ Most recent ER visit was a non-emergency ER visit*

FIGURE 4-3 Non-elderly adults with ER visit in the past 12 months by race/ethnicity, 2008.
NOTE: * = A non-emergency ER visit is one that the respondent says could have been treated by a regular doctor if one had been available.
SOURCE: 2008 Massachusetts Health Insurance Survey.

Disparities Provisions in Chapter 58

Weissman explained that Chapter 58 has three sections that pertain to disparities. First, Section 16O mandates provisions for an ongoing Health Disparities Council. Second, Section 25 describes a pay-for-performance plan, specifically including "the reduction of racial and ethnic health disparities in the provision of care." Third, Section 16L requires the formation of a Health Care Quality and Cost Council (QCC). The QCC is to make recommendations about reducing costs and improving quality of care, as well as on reducing disparities.

Section 16O mandates the development of recommendations for reducing and eliminating racial and ethnic disparities in both access to health care and outcomes. The organization responsible for these recommendations is the Massachusetts Council for the Elimination of Racial and Ethnic Disparities, and it is chaired by two state legislators.

One of the activities of this council is to create a disparities report card. This is an effort to move beyond the situation in which a report is read once and then filed away or put on a shelf. A report card allows continued action and continued accountability. It is essential that the report card be both topical and easily digestible in order to move ahead on reducing disparities. Weissman recommends no more than 20 or 30 indicators for a disparities report card.

Figure 4-4 shows how data beyond the traditional public health statistics can be used to draw attention to a health disparity. For example, although blacks are only 24 percent of the population in Boston, they account for 74 percent of gunshot victims. However, care needs to be taken so that "blaming the victim" does not occur.

The Disparities Report Card for Massachusetts covers the following outline: health status indicators; health utilization, access, and quality indicators; personal health practices and individual factors; social determinants; and laws and social policies affecting health that may disproportionately affect racial and ethnic minorities. One example of such a social policy can be seen in the original creation of the federal Social Security program. When Social Security was started, farm workers and domestic workers were excluded from eligibility. Eighty percent of farm workers and domestic workers were African American at that time. A policy that was in theory designed to be good for all people disproportionately negatively affected racial minorities.

A second example of a policy or regulation that affects minorities is state Medicaid policy. Medicaid underpays physicians for their services. At the same time, racial and ethnic minority group members are disproportionately more likely to use Medicaid. This likely affects access to care for racial and ethnic minority groups.

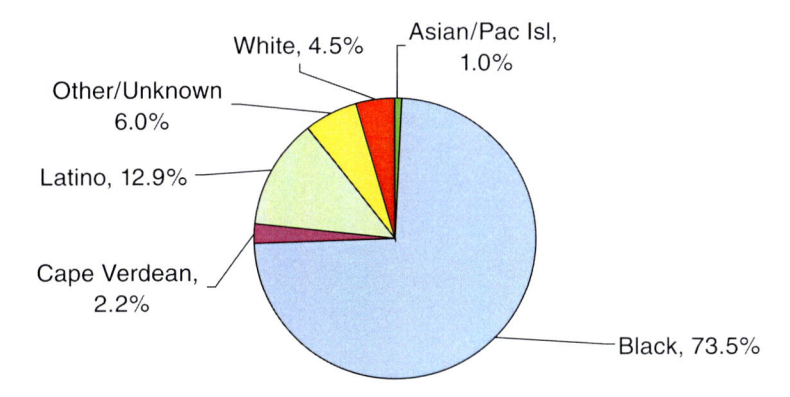

FIGURE 4-4 Nonfatal gunshot injuries by race/ethnicity, Boston, 2003–2005 combined.

Pay-for-Performance Approaches

The second component of health reform, pay for performance (P4P), rewards health care providers for scoring well on certain health indicators in their patient populations. This is another strategy that can be employed to reduce disparities.

Massachusetts uses two types of indicators for P4P. The first involves structural measures, such as culturally linguistic and appropriate services (CLAS). These standards are measured via surveys, and hospitals are rewarded for improving their performance on the CLAS standards.

The second indicator for P4P is clinical measures. Although there are measures that currently exist, the existing measures are targeted for a Medicare population, rather than a Medicaid population. At present, work groups look at measures such as maternity indicators, newborn indicators, and a pediatric asthma indicator. These measures are in the development process so that they better fit a Medicaid population.

Weissman noted that implementation of P4P faces a number of challenges around disparities reduction. The first question is, "Does the measure being used to implement CLAS standards for high-stakes purposes need to be different from the one used for prior reporting?" This can lead to a reexamination of the survey tool in use.

Second, the clinical measures currently in use are based only on Medicaid patients. Does this actually make sense in terms of disparities reduction? It may make more sense to base P4P payments on reducing disparities for all patients, as opposed to just Medicaid patients. This is an issue that will have to be decided in Massachusetts in the future.

The third challenge is the question, "Do Massachusetts hospitals have sufficient numbers of racial and ethnic minority patients for stratification purposes?" Weissman estimated that only 5 to 10 hospitals in Massachusetts actually have sufficient numbers of cases involving racial and ethnic minority patients, making the goal of disparities reduction difficult.

Fourth, Weissman described what he called the "between problem." Disparities not only exist within a health care setting but also exist across the settings themselves. Rewarding particular hospitals, then, for reducing disparities might not actually be targeting the disparities of interest or the settings of interest.

Finally, Weissman discussed the gathering of data on a patient's race, ethnicity, and language (both written and spoken). He emphasized that these data would be a part of the permanent eligibility file rather than included on every claim.

Noting that the collection of these data is controversial, Weissman asked David Pryor, of Aetna, about Aetna's efforts to gather this information for all Aetna patients, as Aetna has been a pioneer in collecting these data. Pryor said that Aetna has approximately 18.5 million members and that data on about 5.2 million of those members have been collected (via self-identification).

Weissman commented that gathering of these data encounters many barriers, including the fact that the process of surveying all health plan members is expensive. His goal was to have health plans collect race and ethnicity data on 2 percent of their members by July 1, 2010. Additionally, the hope is that health plans will begin to see these data to be useful for their own purposes, perhaps increasing the amount of data that they collect.

Indirect estimation is another technique for gauging the race and ethnicity of the target patient population. Developed by Roundtable chair Nicole Lurie and her colleagues at the Rand Corporation, indirect estimation uses the individual's surname and where he or she lives via geocode analysis. These data provide an estimation of the individual's race and ethnicity by providing a probability for each and every possible category. These probabilities are then aggregated. Weissman noted that although both surname analysis and geocoding are not new, it is the combination of the two that allows the estimation to have greater accuracy. For example, a person whose last name is Smith who lives in one area of the city has a different probability of being African American than a person named Smith who lives in a different part of the city.

In one experimental evaluation of the indirect estimation technique, Fremont and colleagues (2005) compared the direct method of determining race and ethnicity (by simply asking patients) with the indirect method (by looking at aggregated health plan data) and found that the indirect method is extremely accurate.

One health plan in Massachusetts used the indirect method to use data to directly affect racial and ethnic health disparities. The Harvard Vanguard health plan has used the indirect method to look at a community where many diabetic patients who were members of minority groups were not getting eye exams. When the plan looked at the community more closely, it was clear that no ophthalmologists practiced in that community. The health plan responded by sending an ophthalmologist into the community to conduct eye exams for the diabetic patients living in that community.

Weissman noted that use of the indirect estimation method sometimes causes discomfort. It is best thought of, he said, as an interim measure. Self-reported race and ethnicity is the "gold standard," but collection of this information is not always feasible. So, in Massachusetts, indirect estimation will be used on a pilot basis with health plans, and the indirect estimation data will be used to supplement, not replace, self-reported data.

Conclusions

The full effects of the Massachusetts health reform plan on the reduction of racial and ethnic health disparities are still unknown. More measurements are needed and more data need to be collected. What is in place, however, is a step in the right direction:

- The Massachusetts Health Disparities Council will release a yearly report card showing the ongoing results of the efforts of the state health care reform program to reduce disparities.
- Mass Health Medicaid is revising and implementing financial incentives to reduce health disparities by race and ethnicity at the hospital level.
- The Quality and Cost Council is poised to make Massachusetts the first state in the nation to stratify HEDIS (Healthcare Effectiveness Data and Information Set) quality measures by race and ethnicity.

DISCUSSION

One workshop participant described the tendency of people to assume that a community that has no local grocery stores is, by definition, a community of color. She questioned, then, why indirect estimation needs to be used to determine this when it is already assumed to be true.

Joel Weissman responded that in large cities, large differences exist between communities within that city; in other words, as he stated, "not all minority communities are the same." The indirect estimation technique has the advantage of allowing more detailed information about a community to be collected. For example, one community may not have adequate bus service for its residents to access health care in a neighboring community. This means that the issues can be better defined and resources can be better targeted to reflect the population of that community.

REFERENCES

Beveridge, W. 1942. *Social insurance and allied services*. Presentation to the Parliament of the United Kingdom, November.

Fremont, A. M., A. Bierman, S. L. Wickstrom, C. E. Bird, M. Shah, J. J. Escarce, T. Horstman, and T. Rector. 2005. Use of geocoding in managed care settings to identify quality disparities. *Health Affairs* 24(2):516–526.

Massachusetts Division of Health Care Finance and Policy. 2008. *2008 Massachusetts Health Insurance Survey*. Boston, MA: Author.

McWilliams, J. M., E. Meara, A. M. Zaslavsky, and J. Z. Ayanian. 2009. Differences in control of cardiovascular disease and diabetes by race, ethnicity, and education: U.S. trends from 1999 to 2006 and effects of Medicare coverage. *Annals of Internal Medicine* 150(8):505–515.

5
Reactor Panel

The final session of the workshop consisted of a panel discussion by three experts who gave their thoughts and reactions to the earlier presentations.

BRIAN SMEDLEY

Brian Smedley is vice president at the Joint Center for Political and Economic Studies and director of its Health Policy Institute. He is also a former Institute of Medicine staff member who worked on the study that culminated in the report *Unequal Treatment: Confronting Racial and Ethnic Disparities in Health Care* (Institute of Medicine, 2003), which examined whether race and ethnicity play a role in predicting the quality of health care (after insurance status and other variables are statistically controlled for).

Smedley noted that some people were quite shocked that *Unequal Treatment* showed that race and ethnicity do play a role: people of color tend to receive lower-quality health care. Numerous published studies in the social science literature demonstrate that these inequalities exist and that racial differences persist in health care in the United States, even when socioeconomic factors are considered. It is critical, then, to look at how and why race is important in predicting who gets what kind of care.

Some readers were less surprised by the findings described in *Unequal Treatment*. When research looking at discrimination in housing opportunities, mortgage lending, and employment hiring is considered, the data are striking. One study demonstrated that when the credentials of two identical job applicants (one African American with no criminal record, one white applicant with a criminal record) were reviewed, the white applicant with a criminal record is even more likely to get hired than the African American applicant (Pager et al., 2009).

More focus on the issue of structural racism is needed, Smedley said. He commented that the reason that it is possible to use indirect estimation (as described in the previous chapter) to predict an individual's race is because white people and people of color live in separate and unequal communities, with people of color concentrated in neighborhoods with high levels of poverty. Regardless of income level, living in a majority African American community means a higher concentration of poverty, few jobs, underresourced schools, fewer grocery stores, and fewer basic services and amenities necessary to enhance health outcomes. This is true even for African Americans with middle or upper levels of income. Residential segregation is a key structural element that must be addressed through state and local strategies to reduce health disparities.

Eliminating racial segregation relies on two different strategies. Place-based strategies can improve investment in low-income communities that suffer from disinvestment. People-based strategies allow people the mobility to move to communities with opportunity. Opportunity programs such as Section 8 housing vouchers are a strategy to accomplish this.

Community health planning is another strategy that state and local authorities can use. Of the few models that exist today, those models have been successful in bringing together a wide range of stakeholders, including health plans, employers, hospitals, other health care systems, and community groups. The goal is to better align the available resources with community needs. Similarly, at the state level, "certificate of need" policies help to keep resources from moving out of those communities that need them most.

Smedley concluded by asking the group how a focus on reports like *Unequal Treatment* can be maintained so that issues of health disparities stay on the table going forward.

WINSTON WONG

Winston Wong is medical director of Community Benefits and director of Disparities Improvement and Quality Initiatives at Kaiser Permanente, an integrated health care delivery system. Kaiser Permanente has 8.7 million members in eight different regions across the country. The focus of Wong's comments was on the personal experience and internal dialogue that people of color experience in confronting racism. He noted that it is not surprising that disparities in health care exist, given that inequities exist in every other aspect of American life. Awareness of health care disparities came about

35 years ago, when the Tuskegee report was released, showing that African Americans were not treated for syphilis so that physicians could study the progression of the disease. The Tuskegee report led the health care community to finally have to admit that disparities exist in health care, just as disparities exist in education and housing.

It is necessary to recognize, however, that physicians alone are not going to change the conditions of inequities in health care. It is a problem that everyone must take responsibility for. As a member of a large integrated health care system, Wong noted that it is necessary to reflect on how as an institution Kaiser Permanente is dealing with the issue of racism. He suggested that an institution like Kaiser Permanente can take three routes: exacerbate the problem, abdicate the problem, or activate the problem.

The health care system exacerbates health care disparities because it is one of the largest polluters in this country: it releases toxic ingredients into the environment, it contributes to the problem of medications in the water supply, and it increases traffic because workers and hospital staff are brought in to build and work in hospitals and health care systems.

Abdication occurs when health care workers believe that because of the existence of social determinants in the environment, they themselves cannot do anything to help people. Activation occurs when a health care system takes some accountability for improving health disparities. Kaiser Permanente and Allina Health Systems are examples of this.

Wong noted that the United States spends 17 percent of its gross domestic product on health care. This means that health care systems control 17 cents of each dollar. This is a major asset, and this means that health care systems should have an impact far beyond that associated with caring for sick people. For example, careful planning needs to go into how hospitals are built and who gets employed, and the fact that the health care system is culpable in reducing or exacerbating health disparities needs to be remembered.

Measurement was the final issue that Wong discussed. He noted that a number of the day's speakers spoke about the importance of measurement. Measurement is necessary to determine the intensity of the disparities, but it is also necessary to measure improvements to interventions to improve disparities. Further efforts are needed in this area, however. For example, when interventions for increasing immunization rates or efforts to reduce the number of infants born with low birth weight are discussed, interventions to increase immunizations are going to be less complicated. Interventions to address low birth weight, by contrast, require several levels of interventions and a multitude of different community partners. A language that can be used to talk about interventions in a consistent and scientific way needs to be developed, Wong said.

Wong concluded by noting that the Kaiser Permanente patient dashboard (a summary of all appropriate patient information that is stored in the electronic health record) is incorporating an "equity button" (to allow patients and staff access to data about racial and ethnic health disparities within the Kaiser system). These data will be reported to the quality improvement group on a regular basis.

ATUM AZZAHIR

Atum Azzahir is the founder of the Phillips-Powderhorn Cultural Wellness Center, a nonprofit organization that functions to provide a place where people can learn their own and each other's cultural traditions around health care practices. The mission of the center is to unleash the power of citizens to heal themselves and build community.

The Cultural Wellness Center was created in 1994. Azzahir noted that because of an award from Blue Cross and Blue Shield for the center's theory of sickness, she feels like the center has been "discovered," and through this discovery, the center has received much support for its activities.

Through a personal tragedy in her own life, Azzahir talked about how what happened is a part of the environment in her community. Her son died at age 47 because of an enlarged heart. As an African American man, the likelihood of him living to be elderly would have been small to begin with. The Cultural Wellness Center attempts to take these feelings of despair and sadness and turn them into knowledge that can be used to build up the community's members.

Azzahir noted that racism was a much discussed topic during the workshop. The Cultural Wellness Center, which has a long history of antiracist work, made a deliberate decision to move from discussing race and racism to talking about culture and cultural resources instead. The primary focus of the center is on healing and recovery both for people of African heritage and for people of native heritage (Dakota and Lakota people).

Other institutions often approach the Cultural Wellness Center to ask whether they may work together as partners. Currently, the center is working to train low-income African Americans to leave the welfare system and obtain meaningful employment. The Cultural Wellness Center sees this as a health care strategy.

From 1994 to 1996, Azzahir went into the community and talked to residents: on the streets, in the park, in kitchens, and on porches. This created the space for a dialogue, and the people she spoke with had much to say. Azzahir spoke to over a thousand people and concluded that loss of community and loss of culture are what make people sick. The Cultural Wellness Center is working on solving this problem so that people may learn how to get healthy. This led to a consideration of questions such as, how do people get well and stay well? And how do people recover from internalized racism? People in the community responded by asking questions such as, "What is community? How do you define community? How do you define culture? How do we take a collective approach?" These are the challenges that the center faced.

In response, a community care giving system was created. The system consists of elders, aunts, uncles, friends, neighbors, and cultures. The birthing teams that are a part of the community care giving system have delivered hundreds of babies. This has led to grandmother support networks where grandmothers are seen as community guardians. Since its beginning, the Cultural Wellness Center has had over 13,000 visits each year, has delivered over 75 babies with organized birthing teams, and has worked with over 750 first-year medical students and over 500 family practice residents.

The center also employs community system navigators that find answers to questions, accompany community members to the doctor, and help them develop ways to work for themselves. This is consistent with the first recommendation in the paper of Larry Cohen, Anthony Iton, Rachel Davis, and Sharon Rodriguez paper, A Time for Opportunity: Local Solutions to Reduce Inequities in Health and Safety (see Appendix A). Azzahir noted that she would add the inclusion of culture to the community: culture, community, and health are all connected.

She further noted that because the process of research is knowledge production, it is essential to include communities and cultural groups. These groups learn from one another, teach one another, and view elders as authorities. This is directly related to the recommendation about instituting culturally and linguistically appropriate screening. The community elders attend physician appointments with patients, they talk with the providers, and they participate in health care-related decision making. In many cultural communities, health care decisions are seen to be family or team decisions. Unfortunately, HIPAA (Health Insurance Portability and Accountability Act) laws sometimes collide with this form of decision making.

Cultural knowledge is also critical when surgical procedures are under discussion. Some types of surgical procedures are taboo for some communities. For example, the Ethiopian and Somali residents of the Phillips-Powderhorn neighborhood are suspicious about organ transplants because they fear the potential "manufacturing" of new limbs. Such beliefs are all a part of the cultural underpinnings of what people believe about the human body.

Azzahir closed her comments by stating that a community care system is needed to operate alongside the health care system. The community care system can help to redefine research and can help to consider prevention approaches based on cultural knowledge systems.

QUESTIONS AND DISCUSSION

Workshop participant Sarah Sensman of the Center for Prevention at Blue Cross and Blue Shield of Minnesota asked the first question following the reactor panel. She noted that the lesbian, gay, bisexual, and transgender (LGBT) community, which has a large presence in Minnesota, also suffers from clear health inequities. For example, over 40 percent of LGBT adults use tobacco. Stigmatization and marginalization are also major problems in this community. She explained that Blue Cross and Blue Shield are working on plans to collect data so that it may reach and better serve the LGBT community.

Saundra Crump of Bioethical Solutions asked about providers. It makes sense, she said, that an insurance plan would want its members to stay healthy because it makes them money, but the providers make money only when their patients are sick.

Winston Wong responded that under health care financing reform, the concept of bundled payments to providers will enable them to work toward better health outcomes overall for patients. This would be in lieu of being reimbursed for each separate procedure. It is unclear at this time whether and how this will mitigate health care disparities, he said; the health care system needs to ensure that a patient's overall clinical outcome is improved by that provider feeling accountable for that patient's care.

Saundra Crump also made the point that health care funding cannot be used for the types of wellness services provided by the Cultural Wellness Center. Wellness and prevention are a part of President Barack Obama's stimulus package, Winston Wong said; this is changing the game around focusing on prevention and wellness rather than sickness.

Echoing these thoughts about prevention and wellness, workshop participant Sam Simmons described the work that he does with Atum Azzahir on a local radio station. He said that they had seen promising results from sharing health information on the radio. Simmons noted that the critical feature is reintegrating culture into the community, and he emphasized the importance of building and sustaining community partnerships.

Patricia Baker from the Connecticut Health Foundation raised the issue of the disparities report card from Joel Weissman's presentation. Baker's foundation issued a state-level report card, and she wondered if the report card was a reflection of the health of the community. How does one ensure that the right outcomes are being measured? Joel Weissman responded that the Seattle, Washington, health department is doing work around healthy communities and that it could serve as a resource. Brian Smedley commented that it is what happens after the report card is issued that is important. It is critical to ensure that resources are tied to the outcomes of report cards.

Joel Weissman discussed the fact that people in the United States no longer think that the nation has the best health care system in the world. European nations, in fact, have better outcomes, better care, fewer health disparities, and greater satisfaction. The United States needs to transform the way that health care is organized and delivered. Simply changing payment systems will not change the health of the community, he said.

Change in the training of physicians is needed as well, Weissman explained. Medical students are not taught how to do population health, how to work with communities, how to work on teams, and how to use community health workers to address local health concerns. The medical home, he said, is a step in this direction.

Atum Azzahir of the Cultural Wellness Center described the center's working relationship with Allina Health Systems. She noted that the system was open to hearing the community's vision for health and its definition of health. It is a partnership, Azzahir said; in this way, members of the community are not made to feel like they are victims. This relationship has made the collection of data community much easier because community members see themselves as the beneficiaries of the data collection process.

Workshop participant Terry Long suggested that the use of a payment system can serve as an incentive for patients to change their behavior. He used the example of his own health plan, which pays him a monthly incentive to exercise a certain number of times per week. This would encourage community members to take charge of their own health and to engage in more positive health behaviors.

Atum Azzahir of the Cultural Wellness Center responded that although this could be a successful strategy, the reasons behind unhealthy behavior also need to be considered. She noted that community members have told her that what makes them want to engage in healthy behaviors and take better care of themselves is having a purpose for living. In other words, behavior change can happen when people feel that they have something to live for.

Larry Cohen, one of the writers of the commissioned paper (see Appendix A), commented that the concept of looking at the culture of a community makes a great deal of sense to him. Using the concept of behavioral norms, he explained that behavior can be changed by changing community norms. For example, before car seat laws for infants and children, less than one in four parents used car seats for their children. When the law passed, implementation of the new policy led virtually all parents to use car seats for their children. This change in policy led to changes in a cultural norm. Building upon this idea of norms, Cohen stated that doctors and medical institutions need to make the community and the members of that community the center of the debate.

Annette Williamson of the Department of Health in England said that the U.S. concept of a health disparities report card was not dissimilar to the "primary care balance score card" used in England. Health in England is increasingly focused upon primary prevention within communities and social capital, an area of potential collaboration for the United States and England. Williamson also said that each local authority and primary care trust conducts an annual joint strategic needs assessment that considers clinical services, social care, and community perspectives to ensure effective targeting of services.

Abebech Mimi Girma of the Cultural Wellness Center suggested that the focus needs to move away from disparities and to health as a whole. For example, everyone is exposed to television advertisements from pharmaceutical companies. Everyone has access to things that are not protected by the Food and Drug Administration. Girma said that those things that make people well spiritually, emotionally, physically, and mentally need to be evaluated.

Jeff Levi raised the issue of the responsibilities of public health agencies to improve the health of a community and its residents. A cultural shift in the field of public health, medicine, and communities is needed. A common definition of "prevention" is also needed.

Levi also brought the conversation back to Sarah Sensman's earlier comments about disparities affecting the LGBT community. He said that the same issues of looking at what "community" means apply. Because some people are too uncomfortable to talk about the reasons and the culture underlying behaviors in the LGBT community, health care is not doing a good job of using prevention strategies to change these behaviors. What is needed, Levi said, is good leadership from the top that forces change in the public health and medical communities.

Roundtable member Jim Kimmey of the Missouri Foundation for Health (MFH) offered a historical perspective on health care reform. In 1994, 1970, and 1912, when health care reform was discussed, the concept of community was not discussed and the existence of health disparities was not recognized. So, the current discussion of health care reform is a very different conversation than the discussions that have taken place over the past 35 or 40 years.

Kimmey also suggested that the role of the philanthropic sector has not been adequately addressed in discussions of health care reform. The philanthropic sector is not constrained by the same things that constrain state and local government agencies. In particular, state and regional foundations can do a number of things to address social determinants of health. For example, MFH provides funding to 84 counties in Missouri and has an endowment of over $820 million.

Roundtable cochair Mildred Thompson mentioned the major initiative funded by the Robert Wood Johnson Foundation to address childhood obesity. She echoed Kimmey's comments and noted that more attention needs to be paid to the role of philanthropy in general.

Atum Azzahir of the Cultural Wellness Center presented another perspective on the philanthropic sector. Because they are informed by data and scientific knowledge, foundations have expected outcomes. Funding, therefore, is dependent on achieving those outcomes. She noted that sometimes their criteria for success are narrower than the community's criteria. It is critical to discuss the research, the outcomes, and the funding when relationships are being built between community organizations and funders.

Workshop participant Helen Bassett raised the issue of health literacy and how important it is to address health literacy when working with community members about health. She noted that the role of health literacy in community capacity "cannot be underestimated" and should be a part of all partnerships between health systems and community organizations.

Health care rationing was discussed by workshop participant Saundra Crump. The health care system cannot afford to give every patient every service, she said, particularly with the large number of aging baby boomers entering the health care system. But this cannot be a top-down decision; it has to occur at the grassroots, community level. Health care systems and the government cannot be making decisions about who gets what.

Larry Cohen noted that rationing does exist de facto in the United States. The United States, he said, rations by price—what people can afford. In response, Annette Williamson said that the National Health Service in the United Kingdom has finite resources and infinite demand; therefore, health care resources are distributed according to need and evidence of impact. A recent example of evidence-based care included the drug tamoxifen, used to treat breast cancer, which was not universally available because of the cost. The National Institute for Clinical Excellence in England (NICE) assessed the evidence surrounding the cost and impact of treatment in relation to the quality of life years gained; NICE has now assessed tamoxifen to be an effective treatment, and it is now widely available. Williamson stated that there must be a rationale and clear evidence in support of resource use and impact/outcome.

CLOSING COMMENTS

Roundtable chair Nicole Lurie ended the day with her final observations about the workshop. The workshop was to accomplish three things. The first, she said, was to highlight how state, local, and international policies can have an impact on racial and ethnic health disparities. By highlighting some promising models and sharing some examples of what works, one can see what is possible. Hearing about how states (Minnesota and Massachusetts) and another country (England) have addressed issues of health care inequities speaks to the importance of the kinds of investments necessary to achieve better health outcomes for all racial and ethnic groups in the future.

Lurie was the director of the Center for Population Health and Health Disparities at the Rand Corporation. The center's research focuses on the role of place in health outcomes, specifically, the effects of a neighborhood's socioeconomic status (SES) and how that differs from both individual attributes (such as gender or education) and individual health behaviors (such as smoking or exercise). Research conducted at the center indicates that for women, the risk of death associated with SES, independent of individual attributes and health behaviors, is about 50 percent higher in poor neighborhoods (those neighborhoods in the lowest SES quartile) than neighborhoods in the highest quartile. Lurie noted that biological markers are associated with living in neighborhoods of high poverty. High levels of stress are common in poor neighborhoods; this, in turn, leads to heightened levels of cortisol in the bloodstream, high blood pressure, and then heart disease. This process, however, is invisible to everyone until the final diagnosis of heart disease is made.

Although the biological processes of stress are invisible, neighborhood conditions are not. Robert Johnson of the Center for Population Health and Health Disparities has studied exposure to neighborhood poverty over the life course. He discovered that exposure to concentrated neighborhood poverty during early childhood is directly predictive of the differences between African Americans and whites in the development of hypertension. The cumulative effects of poverty are even more destructive.

Health care systems, however, are also a part of the neighborhood. They can serve an important leadership role in the community by stimulating the development of policies, partnerships, and investments that can lead to healthier outcomes for everyone. What is interesting is that this occurs less so because of the actual provision of clinical care. Rather, it is the health system's leadership role that is important. Allina Health Systems is a perfect example of this.

Lurie noted that local policies are critical and much easier to influence than federal policies. The federal government is a harder ship to steer, she said. However, it is essential to look at federal policy in terms of health care reform efforts. Insurance coverage for everybody is going to take the country a long way and will have a particularly important impact on early childhood health and wellbeing. There are also creative ideas about payment mechanisms, bundled payments, and different kinds of financing mechanisms that can be linked to incentives. Finally, creation of a "wellness trust" to ensure a continued focus on community prevention has been discussed.

Aside from health care reform efforts, other investments must be considered. Investing in the community and in community prevention efforts is essential. So is investment in early childhood programs; those investments should actually be treated as investments in health. Addressing the environmental determinants of health to improve air and water quality must also occur sooner rather than later. Finally, investments in housing should also be seen as investments in health.

Throughout the workshop, the concept of "building community" was discussed. Using new technologies such as Facebook is another approach to building community that has not been given much thought before. It is another form of community building that needs to be considered.

Lurie closed her comments with a story about community building during the 2008 presidential election. She volunteered in a Philadelphia neighborhood where prior elections had seen much voter intimidation. However, during the 2008 election, this low-income neighborhood was galvanized. The campaign office was incredibly well organized and had an abundance of volunteers who poured in from the streets.

Although it was a very poor neighborhood, Lurie also felt very safe because of the sense of community surrounding the excitement of the election. She spoke with roving groups of adolescents who wanted to know where to get political buttons or how to help. She went door to door to encourage people to vote. Over and over, Lurie said, neighbors were going door to door to help their neighbors vote.

What is important to take away from this story is that these are people who are seen to be "hard to reach" in the public health community. For many of the residents of that Philadelphia neighborhood, they did something they had never done before: they voted, and they encouraged others to vote. This was all community building. This was also the creation of new social networks, new kinds of messaging, and new kinds of communication. The challenge is, how can what was seen in that election be used to transform health? Creative thinking must be given to how to use new tools, new knowledge, and what is already known about community building to improve the health of that neighborhood, that community, and the nation as a whole.

REFERENCES

Institute of Medicine. 2003. *Unequal treatment: Confronting racial and ethnic disparities in health care*. Washington, DC: The National Academies Press.

Pager, D., B. Bonikowski, and B. Western. 2009. Discrimination in a low-wage labor market: A field experiment. *American Sociological Review* 74(5):777–799.

A

A Time of Opportunity: Local Solutions to Reduce Inequities in Health and Safety

A Time of Opportunity:
Local Solutions to Reduce Inequities in Health and Safety

PRESENTED TO THE
Institute of Medicine Roundtable on Health Disparities

Minneapolis, MN
May 2009

Principal authors:
Larry Cohen, MSW, Prevention Institute
Anthony Iton, JD, MD, MPH, Alameda County Public Health Department
Rachel A. Davis, MSW, Prevention Institute
Sharon Rodriguez, BA, Prevention Institute

Prevention Institute is a nonprofit, national center dedicated to improving community health and well-being by building momentum for effective primary prevention. Primary prevention means taking action to build resilience and to prevent problems before they occur. The Institute's work is characterized by a strong commitment to community participation and promotion of equitable health outcomes among all social and economic groups. Since its founding in 1997, the organization has focused on injury and violence prevention, traffic safety, health disparities, nutrition and physical activity, and youth development. This, and other Prevention Institute documents, are available at no cost on our website.

APPENDIX A

Summary of Recommendations

Community Recommendations

- C1 Build the capacity of community members and organizations.
- C2 Instill health and safety considerations into land use and planning decisions.
- C3 Improve safety and accessibility of public transportation, walking, and bicycling.
- C4 Enhance opportunities for physical activity.
- C5 Enhance availability of healthy products and reduce exposure to unhealthy products in underserved communities.
- C6 Support healthy food systems and the health and well-being of farmers and farm workers.
- C7 Increase housing quality, affordability, stability, and proximity to resources.
- C8 Improve air, water, and soil quality.
- C9 Prevent violence using a public health framework.
- C10 Provide arts and culture opportunities in the community.

Health Care Services Recommendations

- HC1 Provide high-quality, affordable health coverage for all.
- HC2 Institute culturally and linguistically appropriate screening, counseling, and health care treatment.
- HC3 Monitor health care models/procedures that are effective in reducing inequities in health and data documenting racial and ethnic differences in care outcomes.
- HC4 Take advantage of emerging technology to support patient care.
- HC5 Provide health care resources in the heart of the community.
- HC6 Promote a Medical Home model.
- HC7 Strengthen the diversity of the health care workforce to ensure that it is reflective and inclusive of the communities it is serving.
- HC8 Ensure participation by patients and the community in health care related decision.
- HC9 Enhance quality of care by improving availability and affordability of critical prevention services.
- HC10 Provide outspoken support for environmental policy change and resources for prevention.

Systems Recommendations

- S1 Enhance leadership and strategy development to reduce inequities in health and safety outcomes.
- S2 Enhance information about the problem and solutions at the state and local levels.
- S3 Establish sustainable funding mechanisms to support community health and prevention.
- S4 Build the capacity of state and local health agencies to understand and lead population-based health equity work.
- S5 Collaborate with multiple fields to ensure that health, safety, and health equity are considered in every relevant decision, action, and policy.
- S6 Expand community mapping and indicators.
- S7 Provide technical assistance and tools to support community-level efforts to address determinants of health and reduce inequities.

Overarching Recommendations

- O1 Develop a national strategy to promote health equity across racial, ethnic, and socioeconomic lines, with specific attention to preventing injury and illness in the first place.
- O2 Provide Federal Resources to support state and local community-based prevention strategies.
- O3 Tackle the inequitable distribution of power, money, and resources—the structural drivers of the conditions of daily life that contribute to inequitable health and safety outcomes—and especially address race, racism, and discrimination in institutions and polices; racial and socioeconomic segregation; and socioeconomic conditions.
- O4 Improve access to quality education and improve educational outcomes.
- O5 Invest in early childhood.

Equitable Health: A Four-Pronged Solution

In Alameda County, where we live and work, an African American child born today in Oakland's flatlands will live an average of 15 years less than a White child born in the Oakland hills neighborhood.[1] Further, for every $12,500 in income difference between families, people in the lower-income family can expect to die a year sooner. Tragically, public health data confirms this same jarring reality all across American cities, suburbs, and rural areas.

Good health is precious. It enables us to enjoy our lives and focus on what is important to us—our families, friends, and communities. It fosters productivity and learning, and it allows us to capitalize on opportunities. However, good health is not experienced evenly across society; heart disease, cancer, diabetes, stroke, injury, and violence occur in higher frequency, earlier, and with greater severity among low-income people and communities of color—especially African Americans, Native Americans, Native Hawaiians, certain Asian groups, and Latinos. (See Appendix A: Inequitable Rates of Morbidity and Mortality.)

Health inequity is related both to a legacy of overt discriminatory actions on the part of government and the larger society, as well as to present day practices and policies of public and private institutions that continue to perpetuate a system of diminished opportunity for certain populations. Poverty, racism, and lack of educational and economic opportunities are among the fundamental determinants of poor health, lack of safety, and health inequities, contributing to chronic stress and building upon one another to create a weathering effect, whereby health greatly reflects cumulative experience rather than chronological age.[2] Further, continued exposure to racism and discrimination may in and of itself exert a great toll on both physical and mental health.[3] Inequities in the distribution of a core set of health-protective resources also perpetuate patterns of poor health.

Historically, African Americans, Native Americans, Alaska Natives, and Native Hawaiians, in particular, have to varying extents had their culture, traditions, and land forcibly taken from them. It is not a mere coincidence that these populations suffer from the most profound health disparities and shortened life expectancies. In many of the low-income and racially segregated places where health disparities abound, a collective sense of hopelessness is pervasive, and social isolation is rampant. This individual- and community-level despair fuels chronic stress, encourages short-term decision making, and increases the inclination towards immediate gratification, which may include tobacco use, substance abuse, poor diet, and physical inactivity.

APPENDIX A

To date, our collective national response has focused on what happens *after* people get sick or injured. Improving the health care system by increasing access and quality remains an integral component of addressing health inequities. At the same time, recent data indicates we must do more. Despite our decades-long investment in launching clinically focused initiatives to reduce health disparities, we have made *virtually no significant progress* in this domain in the United States.[4,5]

Health equity is everyone's issue, and finding solutions will significantly benefit everyone. As the US population becomes increasingly diverse, achieving a healthy, productive nation will depend even more on keeping *all* Americans healthy. An equitable system can drastically lower the cost of health care for all, increase productivity, and reduce the spread of infectious diseases, thus improving everyone's well-being. Last—and most importantly—the idea of equity is based on core American values of fairness and justice. Everyone deserves an equal opportunity to prosper and achieve his or her full potential, and it is our moral imperative to accomplish this.

We can remedy the problem of disparities in health and safety outcomes by creating a new paradigm addressing the needs that are critical to achieving health equity, and the specific challenges that affect integrating solutions into practice and policy. (See Appendix B: Definitions of Health Disparities and Health Inequities.) The first need is for a coherent, sustainable health care system that adequately meets the requirements of the entire US population and of racial and ethnic minorities in particular. The second need is for adequate community prevention strategies that target the factors underpinning why people get sick and injured *in the first place*. These should be integrated to form a unified system for achieving health, safety, and health equity in the US.

In this paper, we propose a set of solutions that are achievable within the local arena. By local, we mean state, regional, and community levels. These solutions not only address the critical needs but also bridge traditional health promotion, disease management, and health care solutions with more upstream work that focuses on preventing illness and injury in the first place. We will outline a composite of community and health care factors that affect health, safety, and mental health and that—most importantly—provide the framework for accomplishing our four-pronged solution:

1. Strengthen communities where people live, work, play, socialize, and learn

2. Enhance opportunities within underserved communities to access high-quality, culturally competent health care with an emphasis on community-oriented and preventive services

3. Strengthen the infrastructure of our health *system* to reduce inequities and enhance the contributions from public health and health care systems

4. Support local efforts through leadership, overarching policies, and through local, state, and national strategy

Policy and institutional practices are the key levers for change. Institutional practices along with public and private policy helped create the inequitable conditions and outcomes confronting us today. Consequently, we need to focus on these areas—in community, business/labor, and government—in order to "unmake" inequitable neighborhood conditions and improve health and safety outcomes. Policies and organizational practices significantly influence the well-being of the community; they affect equitable distribution of its services; and they help shape norms, which, in turn, influence behavior.

POLICY PRINCIPLES

The following policy principles* provide guidance for taking on the challenge of addressing health inequities:

- Understanding and accounting for the **historical forces** that have left a legacy of racism and segregation is key to moving forward with the structural changes needed. A component of addressing these historical forces should consider policy and reform related to immigrant groups—notably Latinos, Asians, and Arab Americans.
- Acknowledging the **cumulative impact of stressful experiences and environments** is crucial. For some families, poverty lasts a lifetime and is perpetuated to next generations, leaving its family members with few opportunities to make healthful decisions.
- **Meaningful public participation** is needed with attention to outreach, follow-through, language, inclusion, and cultural understanding. Government and private funding agencies should actively support efforts to build resident capacity to engage.
- Because of the cumulative impact of multiple stressors, our overall approach should **shift toward changing community conditions** and away from blaming individuals or groups for their disadvantaged status.
- The **social fabric of neighborhoods** needs to be strengthened. Residents need to be connected and supported and feel that they hold power to improve the safety and well-being of their families. All residents need to have a sense of belonging, dignity, and hope.
- While low-income people and people of color face age-old survival issues, **equity solutions** can and should simultaneously respond to the global economy, climate change, and US foreign policy.
- The developmental needs and transitions of **all age groups** should be addressed. While infants, children, youth, adults, and elderly require age-appropriate strategies, the largest investments should be in early life because important foundations of adult health are laid in early childhood.
- **Working across multiple sectors** of government and society is key to making the necessary structural changes. Such work should be in partnership with community advocacy groups that continue to pursue a more equitable society.
- **Measuring and monitoring the impact** of social policy on health to ensure gains in equity is essential. This will include instituting systems to track governmental spending by neighborhood, and tracking changes in measurements of health equity over time and place to help identify the impact of adverse policies and practices.
- **Groups that are the most impacted by inequities must have a voice** in identifying policies that will make a difference as well as in holding government accountable for implementing these policies.
- Eliminating inequities is a huge **opportunity to invest in community**. Inequity among us is not acceptable, and we all stand to gain by eliminating it.

* ADAPTED FROM: *Life and Death From Unnatural Causes: Health & Social Inequity in Alameda County.* Alameda County Public Health Department September 2008.

APPENDIX A

Critical Needs for Achieving Equitable Health in the United States: A Health System

We need a coherent, sustainable health care system that adequately meets the health requirements of the entire US population and of racial and ethnic minorities in particular

When we talk about fixing the health care system in the United States, we assume there is a system that can be improved. The underlying problem, however, is that we have no coherent system in the first place. While there are some elements in place, they are inaccessible to a vast number of people, especially the disenfranchised. The last time the World Health Organization published data on international health ranking in their *World Health Report 2000—Health systems: Improving Performance*, the United States ranked number one in health expenditure per capita but only ranked 37th in overall health system performance.[6] Among industrialized countries, the United States came in 25th out of 30 on infant mortality and 23rd out of 30 on life expectancy.[7] The fact that a growing number of people lack health insurance or *adequate* health insurance has been well documented.[8] Furthermore, even for those *with* adequate access to health care, the system is flawed. For example, medical practitioners' job dissatisfaction rates are growing, and major shortages in nursing and allied health professions are projected.[9]

In a time of financial crisis, we may focus exclusively on reforming the areas of greatest expense in the economy, narrowing in on the cost of specific items as we try to reduce that cost or at least slow its *increase*. Studies have revealed that the dramatic rise in the prevalence of chronic disease is a major factor responsible for growth in US health care spending. [10,11,12] This is a cost that can be reduced through prevention.[13] (See Appendix C: The Economics of Prevention.) Further, our current health care system and its reimbursement structure are not designed to incentivize the necessary community-based prevention and management of chronic disease; thus the system is not meeting the needs of communities across our nation, and health care costs will continue to grow.

As we reform and redesign the health care system, we need to explicitly take the issue of equity into account, since anything done to reformulate how care is delivered can either mitigate or exacerbate the problem of inequity. Therefore, quality improvements to any health care component (e.g., prevention, access, and quality) have to embrace principles of cultural competency, diversity, and equity.

We need to create a coherent, comprehensive, and sustainable health care system that is culturally and linguistically appropriate, affordable, effective, and equally accessible to all people—especially disenfranchised populations. The overall health system should start with community strategies—reducing the likelihood that people will get sick or injured in the first place and helping to maintain the well-being of those who are already sick and injured. The overall system should also offer a full set of services (e.g., medical, dental, mental health, and vision), including screening, diagnostic, and disease management services, within the communities where people live.

America's health care system is neither healthy, caring, nor a system.
WALTER CRONKITE

We need adequate community prevention strategies that target the factors underpinning why people get sick and injured in the first place

Health care is vital but alone it is not enough. The health care system has great strength in its committed providers and in its ever-improving diagnosis, procedures, and medicines. Many formerly fatal diseases are now treatable and even curable. Yet, as important as it is to improve the quality of health care services, it is only part of the solution to improving health and reducing health inequities. Patterns of disease and injury that follow the socioeconomic status gradient would still remain.[14] While health care is vital, there are three reasons why addressing access to and quality of health care services alone will not significantly reduce disparities: 1) Health care is not the primary determinant of health; 2) Health care treats one person at a time; 3) Health care intervention often comes late. (See Appendix D: Reasons why addressing access to and quality of health care alone will not significantly reduce inequities.)

In order to successfully address inequities in health and safety, we must pose the following questions: Why are people getting sick and injured in the first place? What impedes their ability to recuperate? Are their neighborhoods conducive to good health? What products are sold and promoted? Is it easy to get around safely? Is the air and water clean? Are there effective schools and work opportunities? Are there persistent stressors in the environment, and what is the long-term impact of this stress on health?

People's health is strongly influenced by *the overall life odds* of the neighborhood where they live. Indeed, place matters. In many low-income urban and rural communities, whole populations are consigned to shortened, sicker lives. While residential segregation has declined overall since 1960, people of color are increasingly likely to live in high-poverty communities.[15] Racially and economically segregated communities are more likely to have limited economic opportunities, a lack of healthy options for food and physical activity, increased presence of environmental hazards, substandard housing, lower performing schools, higher rates of crime and incarceration, and higher costs for common goods and services (the so-called "poverty tax").[16]

Conversely, people are healthier when their environments are healthier. For example, in African American census tracts, fruit and vegetable consumption increases by 32% for each supermarket.[17] When states moved to require infant car seats, the impact of policy far exceeded that of education in changing norms and thus behavior: usage for infants went from 25% maximum to nearly universal, and death and injury from car crashes decreased.[18]

Taking a step back from a specific disease or injury reveals the behavior (e.g., eating, physical activity, and violence) or exposure (e.g., stressors and air quality) that increases the likelihood of the injury or disease. Through an analysis of the factors contributing to medical conditions that cause people to seek care, researchers have identified a set of nine behaviors and exposures strongly linked to the major causes of death: tobacco, diet and activity patterns, alcohol, microbial agents, toxic agents, firearms, sexual behavior, motor vehicles, and inappropriate drug use.[19] Limiting unhealthy exposures and behaviors enhances health and reduces the likelihood and severity of disease and injury. In fact, these behaviors and exposures are linked to multiple medical diagnoses, and addressing them can improve health broadly. If we take a second step back from the medical conditions, we see that specific elements of the environments in which people live are major determinants of our exposures and behaviors and thus of our illnesses and injuries. (For a more

It is unreasonable to assume that people will change their behavior easily when so many forces in the social, cultural and political environment conspire against such change.
INSTITUTE OF MEDICINE

APPENDIX A

in-depth understanding of this model, please go to Appendix E: A Health Equity Framework:—Taking Two Steps Back to the Determinants of Health.)

Therefore, improving the environments in which people live, work, play, socialize, and learn presents a tremendous opportunity to reduce health inequities by preventing illness and injury *before* their onset. THRIVE (Tool for Health and Resilience in Vulnerable Environments), a research-based framework created by Prevention Institute, offers a way to understand determinants of health at the community level.[20] THRIVE includes a set of three interrelated clusters: equitable opportunity, people, and place. Within these clusters are highlighted key factors that influence health and safety outcomes directly via exposures (e.g., air, water, and soil quality; stressors such as racism) and/or indirectly via behaviors that in turn affect health and safety outcomes (e.g., the availability of healthy food affects nutrition). In addition, the environment also has an influence on people's opportunity to access quality medical services, and these are included as a fourth cluster. On the following page, Table 1: Community Factors Affecting Health, Safety, and Mental Health, presents these four clusters.

Clearly, local solutions to health and safety inequities are central to success. Local work complements broader national change, and local solutions often help shape profound, long-lasting federal changes. Altering community conditions, particularly in low-income communities of color where the memory and legacy of dispossession remains, requires the consent and participation of a critical mass of community residents. Thus strategies that reconnect people to their culture, decrease racism, reduce chronic stress, and offer meaningful opportunities are ultimately health policies. Effective change is highly dependent upon relationships of trust between community members and local institutions. The *process* of inclusion and engaging communities in decision making is as important as the outcomes, which should directly meet the needs of the local population. Strategies such as democratizing health institutions, as was envisioned with the creation of community health centers, foster increased civic participation and serve as a health improvement strategy.

A quality health care system and community prevention are mutually supportive and constitute a health system

While health care and community prevention are often thought of as separate domains and operate independently, they actually are synergistic. Health care institutions have critical roles to play in ensuring an emphasis on health within communities as a key part of the solution. Health services must recognize that the community locale is an essential place for service provision, for example, by expanding community clinics, providing school health services, and giving immunizations in supermarkets. An effective health care institution will also provide broad preventive services, such as screening and disease management, that address populations at-risk and those that already have illnesses.

Health care also has a role to play in improving community environments. It is one of the nation's largest industries and is often the largest employer in a low-income community. As such, health care institutions can support pipeline development to recruit, train, and hire people from the community, especially from underserved sectors. They can also advocate for community changes that will positively impact disease management, such as healthier eating and increased activity; improve the local economy by purchasing local products; create a farm-to-institution program to incorporate fresh, local produce and other foods into cafeteria or patient meals; reduce waste and close incinerators to reduce local pollution; and enhance staff and community access to fresh produce

TABLE 1. Community Factors Affecting Health, Safety, and Mental Health

EQUITABLE OPPORTUNITY
1. **Racial justice**, characterized by policies and organizational practices that foster equitable opportunities and services for all; positive relations among people of different races and ethnic backgrounds
2. **Jobs & local ownership**, characterized by local ownership of assets, including homes and businesses; access to investment opportunities, job availability, and the ability to make a living wage
3. **Education**, characterized by high-quality and available education and literacy development across the lifespan

THE PEOPLE
1. **Social networks & trust**, characterized by strong social ties among persons and positions, built upon mutual obligations; opportunities to exchange information; the ability to enforce standards and administer sanctions
2. **Community engagement & efficacy**, characterized by local/indigenous leadership; involvement in community or social organizations; participation in the political process; willingness to intervene on behalf of the common good
3. **Norms/acceptable behaviors & attitudes**, characterized by regularities in behavior with which people generally conform; standards of behavior that foster disapproval of deviance; the way in which the environment tells people what is okay and not okay

THE PLACE
1. **What's sold & how it's promoted**, characterized by the availability and promotion of safe, healthy, affordable, culturally appropriate products and services (e.g., food, books and school supplies, sports equipment, arts and crafts supplies, and other recreational items); limited promotion and availability, or lack, of potentially harmful products and services (e.g., tobacco, firearms, alcohol, and other drugs)
2. **Look, feel & safety**, characterized by a well-maintained, appealing, clean, and culturally relevant visual and auditory environment; actual and perceived safety
3. **Parks & open space**, characterized by safe, clean, accessible parks; parks that appeal to interests and activities across the lifespan; green space; outdoor space that is accessible to the community; natural/open space that is preserved through the planning process
4. **Getting around**, characterized by availability of safe, reliable, accessible and affordable methods for moving people around, including public transit, walking, and biking
5. **Housing**, characterized by availability of safe, affordable, and available housing
6. **Air, water & soil**, characterized by safe and non-toxic water, soil, indoor and outdoor air, and building materials
7. **Arts & culture**, characterized by abundant opportunities within the community for cultural and artistic expression and participation and for cultural values to be expressed through the arts

HEALTH CARE SERVICES
1. **Preventive services**, characterized by a strong system of primary, preventive health services that are responsive to community needs
2. **Cultural competence**, characterized by patient-centered care that is understanding of and sensitive to different cultures, languages and needs
3. **Access**, characterized by a comprehensive system of health coverage that is simple, affordable and available
4. **Treatment quality, disease management, in-patient services, and alternative medicine**, characterized by effective, timely, and appropriate in-patient and out-patient care including for dental, mental health, and vision
5. **Emergency response**, characterized by timely and appropriate responses in crisis situations that stabilize the situation and link those in need with appropriate follow-up care

by establishing accessible farmers' markets or farm-stand programs. For example, Kaiser Permanente, the nation's largest HMO, has instituted farmers' markets in some of the communities it serves, providing healthy options for the residents, offering a needed place to purchase quality food, and strengthening the nearby local farms.

Equally, community prevention efforts should be a part of the strategy to foster health and reduce health disparities by improving the success of treatment and injury/disease management even after people get sick or injured. Illnesses such as diabetes, cardiovascular disease, HIV/AIDS, and cancer require patients to do what the medical practitioner requests, such as eat healthy foods and be more active. It is important for health care institutions to recognize the ways in which poverty and other social structures impede a patient's ability to follow a doctor's recommendations. Disenfranchised people usually don't have safe places to walk or healthful food to eat. Overwhelmed with the requirements of work and daily life and coping with transportation and childcare issues, poor people can have more obstacles to keeping medical appointments as well. With community prevention efforts bolstering neighborhood environments and support structures, disease management strategies will be more effective.

Challenges to Achieving Health Equity through Practice & Policy

Achieving equitable outcomes is challenging and will take concerted attention, leadership, and investment. Building on interviews with local health officers conducted to inform the development of a Health Equity Toolkit funded by the Robert Wood Johnson Foundation as part of the project *Advancing Public Health Advocacy to Eliminate Health Disparities*, we have identified challenges that officials and communities face. This identification is key to shaping responsive solutions.

1. We haven't embraced the problem of health inequities at its roots

We need to recognize that health inequities are rooted in historical policies and practices and are entrenched in social structures that create barriers to opportunity. This legacy remains invisible to many health care practitioners, policy makers, and the public. Practitioners and community spokespersons need to talk about race and social justice in new ways and often need guidance to do so effectively.

2. We don't have a good playbook for how to do this

The people and institutions working for reform need more guidance and information in order to identify and realize the most effective, sustainable changes. They often lack standardized, comparative data; documented examples of success; protocols for adaptation, with attention to fidelity of core elements; a set of best practices; a framework to measure outcomes and successes; and clear goals for the community.

The roles of different players are not well-defined. Many health issues can be traced to determinants that cross over into other public sectors, such as housing. Public health practitioners have indicated a need for guidance on strategies where public health can take the lead.[21] Further, they don't always know how to coordinate with leadership in other sectors such as housing. In most cases, the charge to address health equity will require public health practitioners to step outside of the contemporary bounds of public health, but this will mean establishing effective communication channels, navigating turf issues, and clarifying shared goals and objectives.

Also, the role of other institutions needs clarification as part of a coherent effort. Banks, businesses, multiple government sectors, schools, and community groups all have a major influence on health equity outcomes, even though they may not realize it or consider it in their decision-making processes. While these players may not see themselves as having an active role, none should be taking actions that are detrimental to health outcomes.

3. A siloed system leads to a fragmented approach at best

Even if there were a shared understanding of the root of health inequities, sectors are siloed without a mechanism to work collaboratively to provide a coherent, effective set of solutions. By and large, there is a lack of coordination and cross-fertilization across sectors, efforts, and disciplines.[22] This is critical to address, because reducing health inequities cannot be achieved by any one organization or sector, let alone any single department or division within public health.

Not only are sectors siloed, but the health system itself is siloed. Even within public health departments, opportunities to create meaningful collaboration across divisions, sections, or departments are limited. Categorical funding—important because it provides dedicated resources to deliver essential programs and services—can reinforce siloed approaches. There is even a divide between public health and health care; the two don't work together systematically and strategically to catalyze, advocate for, and launch the kinds of solutions that can make a fundamental difference. Finally, community members are not consistently included in prioritizing problems or in shaping solutions.

4. Community-based, family-centered primary care is not a medical emphasis

Medical reimbursement, prestige, and medical education norms can all favor specialization over community-based, family-centered primary care. Furthermore, there is a lack of value and incentive placed on allied health professionals, promotoras (i.e., community health workers), and patient navigators. We also need to incentivize preventive services and better train medical providers in prevention.

5. Disparities in health care are not an organizational priority for many US hospitals

Many hospitals consider disparities in care as a function of conditions beyond their control. They may be reluctant to openly address "disparities" collaboratively, because this might be viewed as an admission of inequitable care.[23] Often providers assume they administer equal care since it is their mission. Stratifying their publicly reported quality measures by patient race and ethnicity would be one way to confirm their assumption or identify areas for quality improvement work.

6. Health equity isn't embedded in most people's job descriptions; there are many competing demands

Research and practice in equitable outcomes tend to occur *either* as a small part of one's job or as a specialty focus of a small group of experts within an organization. The challenge here is how to embed health equity into research and practice across and within organizations, bringing these efforts to scale, infusing them into the broader organizational culture, and propelling them to center stage.

APPENDIX A

RECOMMENDATIONS

Local Solutions for Advancing Equity in Health and Safety

Community Recommendations

Strengthen communities where people live, work, play, socialize, and learn

C1 **Build the capacity of community members and organizations.** Capacity building enables the residents and grassroots groups affected by poor health outcomes to better solve the community problems undermining health and safety. Strategies include:

- Train public sector staff to encourage local capacity building and to empower residents to take action in partnership with city and county governments and community-based organizations to improve their neighborhood conditions.
- Invest in both established and developing community organizations. Encourage and strengthen the capacity of these and other institutions and of individuals via financial support, technical assistance, and sharing best practices.
- Foster structured community planning and prioritization efforts to implement neighborhood-level strategies to address unfavorable social conditions.

C2 **Instill health and safety considerations into land use and planning decisions.** Land use, transportation, and community design (the built environment) influence health, including physical activity, nutrition, substance abuse, injuries, mental health, violence, and environmental quality. Strategies include:

- Ensure that health, safety, and health equity are accounted for in General Plans, Master Plans, or Specific Plans; zoning codes, development projects, and land-use policies.
- Engage community residents in developing zoning laws and general plans to integrate health and equity goals and criteria into community design efforts.
- Train public health and health care practitioners to understand land use and planning and to advocate for policies that support health and safety.

Integrating a community health and wellness element into general plans

The city of Richmond, California, is one of the first cities in the country to develop a comprehensive general plan element that addresses the link between public health and community design. Nearly 40% of Richmond's residents live in poverty and over 60% are African American and Latino.[24] This element addresses health impacts of community design decisions, such as zoning, on all Richmond residents as well as the historic impacts on low-income communities and communities of color, which share a disproportionately higher burden of negative health impacts. The General Plan considers factors such as physical activity, nutrition, non-motorized travelers' safety, hazardous materials and contamination, air and water quality, housing quality, preventive medical care, homelessness, and violence, among others.

General plans are mandated for every city and county in California and typically cover a 20- to 30-year time period. Local authorities, either the Planning Commission and City Council for cities, or the Board of Supervisors for counties, must adopt a general plan. In practice, most local authorities appoint committees of residents to inform the process. In California, the Governor's Office of Planning and Research outlines guidance for development of these plans, including the various elements that must be involved. Other states have similar requirements (and often refer to these plans as "Master Plans"). To date, elements directly addressing the health and justice implications of community design have never been included in the guidance but they are gaining attention.

C3 Improve safety and accessibility of public transportation, walking, and bicycling.
Transportation is the means to accessing key destinations such as schools, workplaces, hospitals, and retail venues. Shifting the dominant mode of transportation from driving to greater public transportation use, walking and/or bicycling is a key step to increasing physical activity, reducing traffic injuries, and reducing developmental and respiratory illnesses from poor air quality. Strategies include:

- Implement land-use strategies such as high density, mixed-use zoning, transit-oriented development and interconnected streets that promote walking and bicycling as a means of transportation.
- Adopt complete streets policies in state and local transportation departments to ensure that roads are designed for the safety of *all* travelers including pedestrians, bicyclists, wheelchairs, and motor vehicles.
- Ensure that public transportation options are safe, easily accessible, reliable, and affordable.
- Design public transit routes to connect community residents to grocery stores, health care, and other essential services.
- Prioritize federal transit funding towards biking, walking, and public transportation.

New Jersey Safe Routes to School improvements in vulnerable communities

Safe Routes to School (SRTS) Federal funding gives states and localities a resource for programs that make walking and bicycling conditions safer, more accessible, and more convenient for children and their families. New Jersey Department of Transportation (NJDOT) is carrying out an Urban Demonstration Project in Newark, Trenton, and Camden to identify barriers to applying for and implementing SRTS programs in urban communities. NJDOT engaged students, school officials, and neighborhood partners to develop a needs assessment and a transportation plan that prioritized safe walking and bicycling. Through the community assessment process, NJDOT identified violence and crime, blighted buildings, and traffic safety as key concerns they will now address in the final package of infrastructure and programming improvements, using SRTS resources.

Congress created a $612 million federal SRTS program in the 2005 federal transportation bill to launch efforts from 2005 to 2009. The pending authorization of a new federal transportation bill can be an opportunity to substantially expand the SRTS program.

APPENDIX A

C4 **Enhance opportunities for physical activity.** Home, school, and community environments can either promote or inhibit physical activity. Physical activity is essential to preventing chronic illnesses and promoting physical and mental health. It is imperative to establish a foundation of activity behaviors from an early age and to provide environments with access to parks, open space, and recreational facilities that support people in attaining the daily recommended levels of physical activity.[25] Strategies include:

- Develop and promote safe venues and programming for active recreation. Ensure parks, playgrounds, and playing fields are equitably distributed throughout the community.
- Facilitate after-hour (joint) use of school grounds and gyms to improve community access to physical activity facilities.
- Require recess and adopt physical education policies to ensure all students engage in developmentally appropriate moderate-to-vigorous physical activity on a daily basis.
- Establish state licensing and accreditation requirements/health codes and support implementation of minimum daily minutes of physical activity in after-school programs and childcare settings.

C5 **Enhance availability of healthy products and reduce exposure to unhealthy products in underserved communities.** The food retail environment of a neighborhood—the presence of grocery stores, small markets, street vendors, local restaurants, and farmers' markets—plays a key role in determining access to healthy foods. Communities of color and low-wealth neighborhoods are most often affected by poor access to healthful foods.[26] Research suggests that the scarcity of healthy foods makes it more difficult for residents of low-income neighborhoods to follow a good diet compared with people in wealthier communities.[27] Strategies include:

- Invest in Fresh Food Financing Initiatives to provide grants, low-interest loans, training, and technical assistance to improve or establish grocery stores, small stores, and farmers' markets in underserved areas.
- Encourage neighborhood stores to carry healthy products and reduce shelf space for unhealthy foods through local tax incentives, streamlined permitting, and zoning variances.
- Ensure grocery stores, small stores and farmers' markets are equipped to accept Supplemental Nutrition Assistance Program (SNAP) (formally known as the Food Stamp Program) and Special Supplemental Nutrition Program for Women, Infants, and Children (WIC) benefits.
- Establish and enforce regulations to restrict the number of liquor stores and their hours of operation.

Fresh food financing to enhance the availability of healthy products in underserved communities

In 2004, the Food Trust in Philadelphia, PA, in partnership with The Reinvestment Fund and the Greater Philadelphia Urban Affairs Coalition, identified a strong need for government investment to finance supermarkets, grocery stores, and other healthy food retailers in underserved communities. This led to the first statewide fresh food financing initiative. The Philadelphia Legislature allocated $10 million in its annual appropriations in 2004, with additional funds allocated in 2005 and 2006, to establish a grant and loan program to encourage supermarket development in underserved areas. The Reinvestment Fund leveraged the investment to create a $120 million initiative composed of state dollars, federal tax credit dollars, and private investments. To date, the initiative has provided $63.3 million in grants and loans for healthy retail projects, resulting in the creation of and improvements to 68 stores that offer fresh foods. These projects have generating 3,734 jobs and 1.44 million square feet of floor space.[28] It is now seen as a model and is being replicated in other US communities.

For more information, visit: www.thefoodtrust.org/

C6 **Support healthy food systems and the health and well-being of farmers and farm workers.** What farms grow, how they grow it, and how it gets to the consumer have a profound impact on what we eat, on our health, and on our environment. US farm policy and agricultural research and education have contributed to the proliferation of industrial farms that grow grains, oil seeds, corn, meat, and poultry that serve as raw ingredients for cheap soda, fast food burgers, and other highly processed products. These industrial farms pollute the air, water, and soil while harming our nutritional health. Small- and mid-size farmers are struggling to make a living under the current system. Farmers of color face discrimination in access to loans. Farm workers are exposed to hazardous levels of pesticides,[29] dangerous working conditions, and poor wages and living conditions. Strategies include:

- Support small- and mid-sized farmers, particularly farmers of color, immigrants, and women through grants, technical assistance, and help with land acquisition, marketing, and distribution.
- Establish incentives and resources for growers to produce healthy products, including fruits, vegetables, and foods produced without pesticides, hormones, or non-therapeutic antibiotics.
- Establish policies that support the health and well-being of farm workers, including enforcing occupational safety and health laws and regulations as well as banning pesticides that may pose health risks. Government entities can also facilitate wage increases for farm workers by providing grants and incentives for growers to engage in labor-sharing strategies with other growers.

Linking green renovation standards and health outcomes

The National Center for Healthy Housing in Columbia, Maryland, is using support from the Blue Cross and Blue Shield of Minnesota Foundation to demonstrate how green building principles can improve health. The center is tracking the health impact of the green renovation of an affordable 60-unit apartment complex in Worthington, Minnesota. Residents are primarily low-income minority families employed in the food processing industry.

Results of this project can inform local zoning decisions and building codes. This is the first time the effect of green building principles will be measured against health outcomes over time. Early results include a majority of adults and children reporting improved health in just one year post-renovation. The adults made large, statistically significant improvements in general health, chronic bronchitis, hay fever, sinusitis, hypertension, and asthma. The children made great strides in general health, respiratory allergies, and ear infections. Overall, there were improvements in comfort, safety, and ease of housecleaning.

For more information, visit: www.nchh.org

C7 **Increase housing quality, affordability, stability, and proximity to resources.** High-quality, affordable, stable housing located close to resources leads to reduced exposure to toxins and stress, stronger relationships and willingness to act collectively among neighbors, greater economic security for families, and increased access to services (including health care) and resources (such as parks and supermarkets) that influence health. Strategies include:

- Support transit-oriented development and other policies and zoning practices that incentivize density, mixed-use, and mixed-income development.
- Ensure that housing standards; building permits for new buildings and rehabilitation; and housing inspections include safety and health considerations regarding design, the use of materials, and construction requirements.

APPENDIX A

- Protect affordable housing stock via rent control laws and condominium conversion policies, increase funding for emergency housing assistance, and maintain single room occupancy hotels.
- Support home ownership by creating community land trusts, increasing funds for and utilization of first-time home buyer programs, and establishing inclusionary zoning ordinances.

C8 Improve air, water, and soil quality. Environmental toxins present in air, water, soil, and building materials, including lead in soil and buildings, air pollution from motor vehicle traffic, and water pollutants, such as oil and human waste, have a substantial effect on health. Strategies include:

- Minimize diesel trucks in residential neighborhoods to reduce exposure to diesel particulates.
- Expand monitoring of air and water quality for impact on low-income and vulnerable populations.
- Enforce national water quality standards.
- Strengthen penalties for industrial and agricultural polluters.
- Replicate effective local lead abatement programs.
- Require public health input on air and water pollution impacts in local land use planning and development decisions.

Reducing toxic pollution in West Oakland

For two years, West Oakland residents and community partners worked to research and identify seventeen indicators to monitor environmental, health, and social conditions for their neighborhood. Residents then used the data in the indicators report to issue a formal request that the Bay Area Air Quality Management District (BAAQMD) develop stronger regulations requiring the Red Star Yeast factory (the area's second leading source of toxic emissions) to reduce both pollution and noxious odors. The evidence in the report was also used to build media advocacy, testify at public hearings, and to garner letters demanding regulation and enforcement from the Department of Public Health and local elected officials. The combination of evidence and pressure led BAAQMD to remove the exemptions that had grandfathered Red Star Yeast into antiquated emissions standards.

For more information, visit: www.pacinst.org/reports/environmental_indicators/neighborhood_knowledge_for_change.pdf

C9 Prevent violence using a public health framework. Violence contributes to premature morbidity and mortality and is a barrier to health-promoting activities, such as physical activity, and to economic development. Strategies include:

- Invest in citywide, cross-sector planning and implementation with an emphasis on coordinating services,[30] programming, and capacity building in the most highly impacted neighborhoods, drawing on such tools as the *UNITY RoadMap*.★
- Support local intervention models to reduce the immediate threat of violence, such as the Chicago CeaseFire model.[31]
- Institute changes in clinical and organizational practices in health care settings to support and reinforce community efforts to prevent intimate partner violence, which results in injury and trauma from abuse, contributes to a number of chronic health problems,[32] and disproportionately impacts immigrant women.[33] (See Appendix F: The Role of Health Care Providers in Reducing IPV.)

★ The *UNITY RoadMap* is a resource for cities that maps out effective and sustainable solutions to prevent violence before it occurs. The *UNITY RoadMap* is informed by the findings from a literature review and interviews with violence prevention practitioners, vetted by city representatives and refined based on cities' input. More information on both is available at: www.preventioninstitute.org/UNITY.html

> **Blueprint for Action: Preventing Youth Violence in Minneapolis**
>
> Recognizing that youth violence is a public health issue, the City of Minneapolis developed the *Blueprint for Action: Preventing Youth Violence in Minneapolis*. Using a comprehensive, holistic approach, the Blueprint aims to address the root causes of violence and significantly reduce and prevent youth violence using a combination of public health and law enforcement strategies. Under the leadership of Mayor JT Rybak, the *Blueprint* is the result of an 8-month collaborative process between the city and diverse community stakeholders. The four goals of the *Blueprint* are to:
>
> 1. Connect every youth with a trusted adult;
> 2. Intervene at the first sign that youth are at risk for violence;
> 3. Restore youth who have gone down the wrong path; and
> 4. Unlearn the culture of violence in the community.
>
> Since the implementation of the *Blueprint*, juvenile-related violent crime citywide declined 37% since 2006 and 29% since 2007.[34] In four of the five targeted neighborhoods, rates declined 43% in 2006 and 39% since 2007.[35] Additionally, the City of Minneapolis has provided over twelve community organizations with grants to support youth employment, academic enrichment, and other community-based programs. Currently, the city has developed a youth violence prevention legislative agenda, which calls for a statewide policy that defines youth violence as a public health issue. It is a member of the UNITY City Network, a public health initiative funded by the US Centers for Disease Control and Prevention.
>
> For more information, please see: www.ci.minneapolis.mn.us/dhfs/yv.asp for *Blueprint for Action: Preventing Youth Violence in Minneapolis* and http://preventioninstitute.org/UNITY.html for *UNITY: Urban Networks to Increase Thriving Youth*.

C10 **Provide arts and culture opportunities in the community.** Artistic and cultural institutions have been linked with lower delinquency and truancy rates in several urban communities,[36] and participation in the arts has been associated with academic achievement, election to class office, school attendance,[37] appropriate expression of anger, effective communication, increased ability to work on tasks, less engagement in delinquent behavior, fewer court referrals, improved attitudes and self-esteem, greater self-efficacy, and greater resistance to peer pressure.[38] Strategies include:

- Support community art centers and other opportunities for creativity in the community.
- Integrate art and creative opportunities into existing programs and businesses.
- House art commissions within state or city government.
- Work with large art institutions, local policy makers, and residents to bring "Big Art" (e.g., museums and orchestras) to low- and middle-income communities.
- Implement a policy to receive a portion of every ticket sold in the community for movies, sporting events, etc. as an alternate source of funding for arts and culture. Another funding mechanism involves redirecting a portion of hotel and car rental taxes, since art contributes to enhancing the community.

APPENDIX A

Philadelphia's Mural Arts Project

The Mural Arts Project (MAP) in Philadelphia has created 2,500 murals citywide. These murals have transformed otherwise depressed and blight-filled neighborhoods throughout Philadelphia into public art displays that cultivate neighborhood pride and reflect the culture, history, and vision of the communities in which they were created.

MAP is an offshoot of the Anti-Graffiti Network, an already existing program intended to provide alternatives to young people engaged in graffiti and other crime. Launched by former Philadelphia Mayor Wilson Goode in 1984, MAP became institutionalized within the city's Department of Recreation more than ten years ago, and in this role it has created new partnerships among government agencies, educational institutions, corporations, and philanthropic foundations to bring murals to fruition. This program trains thousands of youth every year and provides them with the skills to contribute to the aesthetic of their own neighborhoods. It offers an alternative to gangs and a place to receive mentorship from working artists. More recently, in addition to working with youth, The Mural Arts Program began offering a wide array of mural-making programs for adult men and women at correctional facilities in Pennsylvania's State Correctional Institution (SCI) and several sites within the Philadelphia Prison System.

In 1971, Seattle, Washington, established an Arts Commission by ordinance and issued a subsequent ordinance requiring all infrastructure projects to set aside 1% of their project costs for public art. Seattle is a national leader in providing residents and visitors with experiences in public art.

Health Care Services

Enhance opportunities within underserved communities to access high-quality, culturally competent health care with an emphasis on community-oriented and preventive services

HC 1 **Provide high-quality, affordable health coverage for all.** Everyone, including the most vulnerable populations, should have equal access to health care, including medical, dental, vision, and mental health services. There are a disproportionate number of racial and ethnic minorities who either do not have any health insurance or are enrolled in "lower-end" health plans.[39] Strategies include:

- Equalize access to high-quality health plans to limit fragmentation of health care services. For example, Medicaid beneficiaries should be able to access the same health services as privately insured patients.[40]
- Ensure that all eligible children and families enroll in and access the State Children's Health Insurance Program (SCHIP).
- Support safety net hospitals through state insurance coverage and state and local subsidies.[41]
- Ensure equitable support for dental and mental health services.
- Improve access through equitable and fair sharing of health care costs; streamline public health insurance enrollment and increase affordability of services within existing public programs, such as Medicaid; evaluate outreach to and enrollment of underserved populations; and support state and local legislative proposals for universal access to quality health care.

Health care coverage in Massachusetts[42]

Massachusetts's Chapter 58 of the Acts of 2006 provides near-universal health insurance coverage and aims to ensure that all state residents have health insurance options that provide "minimal creditable coverage." The law also has several key provisions that directly and indirectly address disparities in health care. Provisions include:
- Subsidizing health premiums for residents whose incomes fall below 300% of the Federal Poverty Level;
- Charging a new state entity, the Connector, to negotiate with health plans to increase the affordability of unsubsidized coverage and maximize the enrollment of low-income uninsured residents;
- Promoting the diversity and cultural and linguistic competence of health care professionals by establishing a Health Disparities Council in the Office of Minority Health;

Strengthening the data collection and monitoring of disparities through a Health Care Quality and Cost Council within the State Office of Health and Human Services charged with reducing racial and ethnic health disparities and publicly reporting disparities data.

HC2 **Institute culturally and linguistically appropriate screening, counseling, and health care treatment.** Culture shapes beliefs, behavior, and expectations surrounding health and health care. Physicians and other health care providers should deliver quality services in a culturally competent and sensitive manner. This approach can increase patient satisfaction, patient adherence to treatment plans, and the probability of improved health outcomes. Strategies include:

- Adopt standards of practice that are sensitive to the language and cultural needs of all patients.
- Provide training for providers to conduct screening, counseling, and treatment in both a culturally appropriate and sensitive manner.
- Promote culturally and linguistically appropriate screening programs for specific populations, such as Asian women for cervical cancer and other targeted groups for breast and cervical cancer.
- Ensure an effective communication strategy that takes into account the patient's health literacy and preferred language.
- Ensure patient-system concordance (i.e., a setting of care delivery that optimizes patient adherence and a sense of security and safety).

California's Health Care Language Assistance Act[43]

The first of its kind in the country, SB853 holds health plans accountable for the provision of linguistically appropriate services and requires the California Department of Managed Health Care to develop standards for interpreter services, translation of materials, and the collection of race, ethnicity, and language data. The bill was sponsored by the California Pan Ethnic Health Network. The law went into full effect on January 1, 2009.

Summary of SB 853 and its regulations:
1. Health plans must conduct a needs assessment to calculate threshold languages and collect race, ethnicity, and language data of their enrollees.
2. Health plans must provide quality, accessible, and timely access to interpreters at all points of contact and at no cost to the enrollee.
3. Health plans must translate vital documents into threshold languages.
4. Health plans must ensure interpreters are trained and competent and that translated materials are of high quality.
5. Health plans must notify their enrollees of the availability of no cost interpreter and translation services.
6. Health plans must train staff on language access policies and procedures and on working with interpreters and limited English proficiency patients.

> **Non-traditional approaches to improving immigrant mental health and social adjustment**
>
> This concerns how well both immigrants and their receiving communities are able to draw on their strengths and overcome the challenges affecting the health and vitality of entire communities. Recognizing that social capital/connectedness is a determinant of health, the Blue Cross and Blue Shield of Minnesota Foundation created Healthy Together: Creating Community with New Americans, a statewide grantmaking initiative to reduce health disparities for immigrants and refugees, supporting more than 140 projects since 2005. This effort can serve as a model for institutions and governments across the nation. Some promising strategies include:
>
> - Helping new immigrants forge social connections and rebuild the sense of community they may have lost by connecting them to others facing similar issues and creating social gatherings through "Talking Circles."
> - Providing information and education and pursuing other means to "normalize" and remove stigma and misconceptions from mental health issues and treatment.
> - Building on client's strengths, helping them to reframe their experiences as survivors rather than as victims and to create their own solutions.
> - Building cultural competence of providers to recognize mind/body connections and focus on symptoms.
>
> The report is available online at www.bcbsmnfoundation.org

HC3 **Monitor health care models/procedures that are effective in reducing inequities in health and data documenting racial and ethnic differences in care outcomes.** Detailed documentation of health care models/procedures will delineate the key elements of success. Currently, hospital practices for data collection vary widely as do the racial and ethnic classifications used. Strategies include:

- Standardize data: Collect race and ethnicity data in all health institutions. Coordinate state standards for data collection on race and ethnicity with federal standards to track the health of minorities.[44] Although it may be difficult to use data to compare institution-to-institution, hospitals can use it to identify existing disparities in care and track trends for different patient populations within a hospital.
- Coordinate data collection and data systems beyond individual institutions and the health care system: Multiple partners from various sectors should be involved in outreach to different populations. For example, when addressing asthma management, school systems would be able to reach out to a broad range of school-aged children. Public health can play a key role in coordinating data collection at the community level and comparing it across systems.
- Disaggregate the data: Ensure that data reflects differences within the broad categories of race and ethnicity (particularly among Latino and Asian/Pacific Islander populations), as well as income levels, and duration of residence in the United States. Adopt uniform patient classifications in health information technology to make quality analysis easier and quicker. Analysis should be included in quality improvement initiatives.
- Incorporate new accreditation standards and mandates that account for equitable health care.
- Apply emerging data practices to better determine what medical procedures are most effective for different populations. (One size does not necessarily fit all.) Explore the Expecting Success disparities collaborative as one such example. Upon submission of their LOI, although the majority (97%) of the 122 hospitals were collecting patient race and ethnicity data, almost none reported using the data for quality improvement purposes at that time. Currently, they are among the most likely to have begun using quality data to reduce inequities in care.[45]

HC4 Take advantage of emerging technology to support patient care. Recent advances in health care technology can strengthen medical treatment. To the extent that technology is used as an element of quality medical care, it's important to ensure that these advances fully benefit everyone. Cell phones are one area where there is a high degree of market penetration among all groups and so we should capture their potential to support medical treatment so as not to exacerbate disparities. When technology is not equally available (e.g., computers in every home), alternatives should be provided that are efficacious. Strategies include:

- Institute electronic health records that protect privacy but ensure caregivers have all needed information.
- Use telephone and email reminders to increase frequency of appointments and testing compliance, reduce failure to take pills, and encourage following procedures.
- Make tailored health information easily accessible and responsive.

> **Automated Telephone Self-Management Support System (ATSM)**[46]
>
> The Improving Diabetes Efforts across Language and Literacy (IDEALL) Project, run out of the California Diabetes Prevention and Control Program, is successfully utilizing health information technology as an efficient patient-centered approach to diabetes management for underserved populations with communication barriers such as limited literacy and limited English proficiency.[47]
>
> IDEALL compared the effectiveness of two diabetes self-management support interventions (ATSM system and group medical visit support system) against the standard diabetes management approach. More than half of the participants had limited English proficiency, more than half had limited literacy, and half were uninsured. Participants in the ATSM group had the highest levels of participation and showed better communication with providers as compared to usual care and group medical visits. The ATSM participants also demonstrated significant increases in physical activity, exhibited the greatest improvements in carrying out daily activities, and spent fewer days in bed due to illness. Tailored to individual language and literacy need, the ATSM is a cost-effective intervention with great potential for underserved diabetes patients with low literacy and English proficiency levels.[48]
>
> For more information, contact Dean Schillinger, MD, dschillinger@medsfgh.ucsf.edu

HC5 Provide health care resources in the heart of the community. Strengthening the presence of health care services located in communities of high need reinforces the connection between health care and community and can remove pervasive access barriers such as inadequate transportation options or not being able to seek health care during traditional working hours. Strategies include:

- Support community-based clinics. Clinics have an essential role in improving community health and providing services for uninsured and underserved populations. Clinics should establish organizational practices to increase access to equitable health care.
- Expand availability of school-based health clinics.
- Provide support groups that enhance self-efficacy in engaging in healthy behaviors.
- Provide culturally appropriate care such as translation services, disease prevention counseling, advocacy for quality health care, and other services to patients directly in the community, not just in health care settings.
- Expand the use of community health workers. Reforming reimbursement is essential, including state grants and seed funding as resources.[49]
- Change the available work hours and locations to meet the needs of patients.

Project Brotherhood in Chicago, Illinois

Supported by seed money from the Cook County Hospital, Project Brotherhood opened its doors as a health and human services provider to African American men in Chicago in 1998. With support from the Cook County Bureau of Health Services Health Center, Project Brotherhood provides services for men on a drop-in basis. Its explicit mission is to address the physical and mental health needs of a neglected population of Black men in a culturally relevant manner. There is no need for an appointment for physicals or lab tests, which are often needed in order to gain employment. Both primary and specialty health care are provided for free, allowing the low-income men that Project Brotherhood primarily serves to access high-quality, culturally appropriate health care that has historically been inaccessible. To increase levels of initial trust, the majority of staff is both African American and male, services are delivered in a less formal environment by offering weekly casual evenings where doctors, staff, and clients participate in informal support group discussions, and a barber provides free haircuts and counseling.

Project Brotherhood continues to grow the number of patients it is reaching with its services:[50]

- In 1999, Project Brotherhood averaged 4 medical visits and 8 group participants a week.
- By 2005, they averaged 27 medical visits and 35 group participants a week—and 14 haircuts per clinic session.
- No show rates of Project Brotherhood medical visits average 30% per clinic session compared to 41% at the main health clinic.
- By 2007, Project Brotherhood provided services to more than 13,000 Black men.

On Lok Senior Health Services

With support from the City of San Francisco, in 1983, On Lok Senior Health Services obtained waivers from Medicare and Medicaid to test a new financing method for long-term care. In exchange for fixed monthly payments from Medicare and Medicaid for each enrollee, On Lok was responsible for delivering the full range of healthcare services. This model served as a prototype for a national initiative passed in the Balanced Budget Act of 1997—the Program of All-Inclusive Care for the Elderly (PACE), which receives funding from both Medicare and Medicaid and provides an alternative to the traditional nursing home model for elder care. As a certified PACE program, On Lok seniors who are both Medicare and Medi-Cal (Medicaid in California) beneficiaries receive comprehensive health and health-related services with no premiums or co-payments. Supplemental Security Income Program (SSI) benefits can also be contributed to the cost of On Lok services. For seniors who are only Medicare beneficiaries, the cost of services not covered by Medicare are paid for out-of-pocket and are determined by personal income and assets. Its main goal is to keep seniors at home living in their communities for as long as possible. On Lok's services encompass full medical care, prescription drugs, home care, adult day health, transportation, and more. On Lok, means "peaceful, happy home" in Cantonese, the language spoken by most of its elderly participants. Although it is rooted in Chinese cultural traditions of reverence for elders, the program long ago branched out to serve other ethnic and racial groups.[51] In expanding its services to various neighborhoods, a paramount consideration is the culture of the community it is serving.

HC6 **Promote a medical home model.** Having a designated health provider for every patient and, ideally, every family has enormous benefits. Primary care becomes more accessible, continuous, comprehensive, family-centered, coordinated, compassionate, and culturally effective. Patient-centered care is given within a community and cultural context. In 2007, the American Academy of Family Physicians, American Academy of Pediatrics, American College of Physicians, and American Osteopathic Association released the Joint Principles of the Patient-Centered Medical Home. Far fewer people of color have a medical home, which is strongly associated with prevention, screening, and specialty care referral.[52] Strategies include:

- Design interventions to incorporate detection, prevention, and management of chronic disease with full deployment of multi-disciplinary teams that are family and patient centered.

HC7 **Strengthen the diversity of the health care workforce to ensure that it is reflective and inclusive of the communities it is serving.** The diversity of health care professionals is associated with increased access to and satisfaction of care among patients of color. States can adopt strategies such as loan repayment programs and service grants, health profession pipeline programs, and other incentives for service.[53] Strategies include:

- Train clinic providers to conduct culturally appropriate outreach and services.
- Address the imbalance of health care providers by offering incentives to work in underserved communities.[54] States could provide incentives that include funding graduate medical programs focusing on underserved populations, tuition reimbursement, and loan forgiveness programs that require service in Health Professional Shortage Areas (HPSAs).
- Expand use of Community Health Workers (CHWs) as a means of diversification. By acting as health connectors for populations that have traditionally lacked access to adequate health care, CHWs meet the ever-changing health needs of a growing and diverse population. Their unique ties to the communities where they work allow CHWs to understand cultural and linguistic needs and provide a resource for populations that are not necessarily connected or trusting of the medical system.

Invest in community health workers

The State of Kentucky dedicates $2 million annually for Kentucky Homeplace, an initiative that relies substantially on approximately 40 trained Community Health Workers (CHWs)* to deliver services to rural, underserved populations in 58 counties. Similarly, the City of Fort Worth, Texas, has permanently budgeted for 12 community health worker positions within their Department of Public Health. These particular CHWs are based in neighborhood police stations and work on teams with nurses and social workers responding to non-urgent health and social issues from the community at large. The City also supports the CHWs with training and with addressing issues of health disparities.

For nearly a decade, the Blue Cross and Blue Shield of Minnesota Foundation has served as a catalyst to promote the training and use of CHWs. The foundation's support has led to:

- Sustainable financing—Minnesota is the only state, other than Alaska, to obtain Medicaid reimbursement for CHW services.
- An 11-credit CHW certificate program based in the community college system.
- Peer learning and professional development through the Minnesota CHW Peer Network.
- A workforce development partnership through the Minnesota CHW Policy Council.
- Awareness building through a public television program and accompanying DVD.
- CHW models with a current focus on mental health.
- Health plan uptake at Blue Cross and Blue Shield of Minnesota through a CHW internship.

For further information on certain CHW services, visit www.mnchwinstitute.org/MN_Legislation.asp

* CHWs are also known as Lay Health Workers, Promotoras de Salud, Outreach Workers, or Community Health Advocates.

APPENDIX A

HC8 **Ensure participation by patients and the community in health care related decisions.** Research suggests that the consistency and stability of the relationship between patient and doctor is an important determinant of patient satisfaction and access to care. However, people of color are less likely to have a consistent relationship with a provider, even when insured at the same levels as White patients.[55] Strategies include:

- Develop and strengthen patient education programs to help patients navigate the health care system.[56]
- Promote community health planning, which actively involves community residents in planning, evaluation, and implementation of health care efforts.[57]

Senior Injury Prevention Partnership (SIPP)

The population over age 60 will more than double nationally in the next 20 years. In 2005, people age 65 and older represented a little more than 10% of the population of Alameda County but accounted for more than 45% of all hospitalizations and deaths due to unintentional injury.[58] Traditionally, injury prevention programs have focused primarily on children. The Senior Injury Prevention Partnership (SIPP), formed more than 10 years ago by the Alameda County Public Health Department and a diverse array of partner organizations, addresses the needs of the older population in our county. SIPP promotes a multi-factorial fall-prevention program that includes: physical activity, home safety, education, and medication management. SIPP got its start with state and foundation grant funding. Following its initial success and advocacy by seniors, local government funding was also allocated. SIPP trains clinicians working with adults age 65 and over. Their program goes beyond the typical boundaries of the traditional medical model by putting peer-led physical activity programs into place, which have proven to be as or more effective than programs led by clinicians.[59] SIPP is currently hosting trainings for physical activity "lay leaders"—who are often older adults themselves—at senior centers, residential facilities, and other independent senior living locations. By bringing physical activity programs to seniors (rather than the other way around), SIPP increases the likelihood of participation and helps make the healthy choice the easy choice.

HC9 **Enhance quality of care by improving availability and affordability of critical prevention services.** Access to culturally competent, accessible clinical preventative services is a key ingredient to keeping people healthy. Examples include:

- Immunizations of children, adults and seniors.
- Regular monitoring of children's growth.
- Assessment of prevention and safety behaviors (e.g., alcohol, tobacco, gun use; vehicle safety devices; family violence; risks including guns, STD's).
- Medical testing and screening.
- Patient education, counseling, and referrals (e.g., smoking cessation, dietary counseling, and physical activity programs).
- Oral health, a key element of medical care that is too often overlooked.

A community-driven project to reduce STDs in Minneapolis[60]

Based in Minneapolis, MN, Seen on da Streets is a collaborative sexual health program targeting young African American males age 15 to 24 to reduce the prevalence of sexually transmitted diseases (STDs). The Seen on da Streets project is supported by a 5-year research grant from the US Department of Health and Human Services, Office of Population Affairs/Office of Family Planning. The federal support for the project totals $1,406,500 (97.7% of total costs) and the City of Minneapolis' Department of Health and Family Support in-kind contribution totals $33,075 (2.3% of total costs). Additionally, Seen on da Streets received a $12,500 grant from the Community Capitol Alliance to add outreach services to young Latino men. Young adults, people of color, and low-income residents in Minneapolis are disproportionately impacted by STDs and unintended pregnancies, and young adult men in particular are far less likely to receive routine STD screening. Collaborating with two local clinics, the Minneapolis Department of Health hires young people of color from the most impacted communities to provide STD prevention education, risk assessment, and specimen collection for testing. By focusing the outreach on places where young men of color naturally congregate—including city parks, churches, barber shops, street corners, and job training centers—Seen on da Streets has over five years reached over 11,000 young people who would otherwise not have sought care. Over the course of the project, Chlamydia rates have only risen by only 2% in Minneapolis compared to 33% in other parts of Minnesota.

HC10 Provide outspoken support for environmental policy change and resources for prevention. In order to reduce racial and ethnic disparities, public policies and practices must address factors beyond medical care that impact health outcomes and disparities, specifically the community recommendations in this document. Strategies include:

- Advocate for community changes that will improve health outcomes and support disease management by speaking up in the media, community, and political environments and within health care institutions and associations and the broader health care community.
- Support pipeline development to recruit, train, and hire people from the community, especially from underserved sectors.
- Reduce waste and close incinerators to reduce local pollution.
- Purchase products and services from local businesses and organizations, such as food from nearby farms.
- Be attentive to community impact (e.g., reducing noise and emphasizing public transportation).

APPENDIX A 85

Systems Recommendations

Strengthen the health system infrastructure to reduce inequities and enhance the contributions from public health and health care systems

S1 **Enhance leadership and strategy development to reduce inequities in health and safety outcomes.** High level leadership at state and local levels and clear strategic direction are essential to achieving equitable health outcomes. Strategies include:

- Engage civic leadership at the highest levels (e.g., mayors and governors) to coalesce influential partners, establish the priority of reducing inequities, ensure accountability, and use the bully pulpit to elevate the problem and solutions.
- Develop local and state plans that clarify what prioritized actions will be taken in order to achieve health equity.

Mayor's Task Force Blueprint—A plan to eliminate racial and ethnic disparities in health

Boston Mayor Menino convened a blue ribbon task force, composed of leaders from academic institutions, community coalitions, health care, and insurance providers, to develop a blueprint of strategies that address social determinants and health factors that contribute to health disparities. The Boston Blueprint is divided into two sections: 1) Health Care and Public Health and 2) Environmental and Societal Factors. Each section includes specific recommendations and short-term and intermediate action steps.[61] The Boston Health Commission issues progress reports that include a review of successes, lessons learned, and next steps. According to the Year One report, "Large numbers of Bostonians became educated about and involved in the issue of racial and ethnic health disparities. A platform for understanding and engagement has been set. Numerous health and social service agencies trained staff and mounted programs that paved the way for improved services to help reduce disparities in health status. There are notable outcomes from those efforts, including standardized disparities-related data collection in hospital settings, expanded health care quality improvement activities, enhanced patient navigation models, and innovative workforce development efforts."[62]

S2 **Enhance information about the problem and solutions at the state and local levels.** A central challenge of 21st century American health policy is to characterize the powerful relationship between social inequities and health inequities and to identify comprehensive multi-disciplinary community-level interventions that systematically reduce social inequity. Strategies include:

- Develop, test, and disseminate new tools such as Connecticut's Health Equity Index, BARHII's social gradient analyses, San Francisco's Healthy Development Measurement Tool, and other innovative tools that integrate information from varied domains to illuminate relationships between social measures and health status.
- Invest in better communicating the problem so that the general public and potential partners understand the underlying contributors to disparities and can evaluate the broader elements and potential solutions (e.g., the PBS documentary series, *Unnatural Causes—Is Inequality Making Us Sick?*)

> **Faith-based organizing for health equity**
>
> ISAIAH, a faith-based organization committed to racial and economic justice within 100 congregations in Minneapolis, St. Paul, and St. Cloud, Minnesota, is a vehicle for people of faith to work towards creating racially and economically just communities. This work requires that community members have the power to affect the underlying conditions that have an impact on the health of their communities.
>
> Since 2008, ISAIAH has used the PBS series, *Unnatural Causes—Is Inequality Making Us Sick?*—in facilitated screenings. Twenty-seven ISAIAH congregations viewed the series with a guide adapted to include faith reflections and then held conversations with their local officials and 48 state legislators to create a new and uncommon conversation about health. The chair of the Senate Health Policy Committee hosted a viewing of the series, and the Service Employees International Union (SEIU) showed the series to health care workers.
>
> Jewish Community Action and ISAIAH partnered to have an interfaith event with a synagogue, a catholic church, and a Unitarian church with the Senate Finance Committee Chair to introduce the Minnesota Healthy Communities Act, which was co-created by ISAIAH, SEIU, and the Minnesota Public Health Association. The Act includes a community-driven health impact assessment component.

S3 Establish sustainable funding mechanisms to support community health and prevention. Prevention rarely rises to the level of urgency that would support adequate funding, because public budgets remain in crisis mode and the pay off from prevention comes two or five or ten years down the road. Strategies include:

- Educate the broad public about the cost savings of health care and government investments in prevention.
- Create a wellness trust to collect, manage, and expend prevention funding, including indexing prevention to health care costs.
- Reinvest prevention savings in further prevention efforts.

S4 Build the capacity of state and local health agencies to understand and lead population-based health equity work. Having a public health workforce that is equipped to address issues of health equity and to convene key partners is a critical component of success. Public health practitioners have expressed an eagerness to address health equity and social justice along with an awareness that organizational support and staff capacity are crucial to moving this forward.[63] Strategies include:

- Build the capacity of health departments to address issues of equity, including retraining and re-pooling of all staff working in public health and health service to have a solid grounding in the social determinants of health, health equity, and how to work with diverse sectors.
- Recruit and build a diverse health workforce reflective of underserved communities: Institute health equity studies in public health graduate programs; emphasize community-based equity work as a core public health competency and hiring criteria; build a diverse leadership team that includes people most affected; and develop pathways and pipelines for public health professionals to move from community-based equity work into leadership positions.
- Bolster Offices of Minority Health to support multiple sectors/efforts by serving as convener and coordinator of work that spans multiple departments and agencies; providing data sets that help inform and track progress; providing information on most effective practices and solutions;

APPENDIX A

developing policy solutions to be implemented by multiple sectors; and providing training and capacity building to support communities, public health, and other sectors to reduce inequities in health.

S5 Collaborate with multiple fields to ensure that health, safety, and health equity are considered in every relevant decision, action, and policy. Ensuring health in every policy will be essential in significantly improving health and safety outcomes and achieving health equity. Strategies include:

- Engage and coordinate the efforts of multiple sectors and diverse government agencies (e.g., business, labor, educators, public health, housing, transportation, environmental protection, and planning) to establish policies and efforts in support of health equity, including reducing barriers and improving incentives.
- Establish health and health equity impact/analyses: Evaluate proposed policies and funding streams with a "health lens" to determine impact on health, safety, and equity and ensure that consideration of health equity runs through all practices and policies within health institutions and beyond.

> **Washington State's health care expansion laws address health disparities**[64]
>
> In 2006, the legislature in the state of Washington passed four bills addressing the health needs of communities of color, including the establishment of a Governor's Interagency Coordinating Council on Health Disparities, biennial surveys on the diversity of the health care workforce, and review of the health disparities impact of pending laws. The council's charge includes planning for the elimination of disparities in health and collaborating on health impact reviews. In 2007, the legislature took further steps by passing a package of three bills that move the state closer to universal health coverage and also address the health needs of communities of color by:
>
> - Aligning the state's health care resources with community needs, including a particular focus on community and migrant health clinics; and
> - Requiring a "statewide health resources strategy" to survey state demographics, inventory health facilities, and assess health care needs geographically.

S6 Expand community mapping and indicators. Community mapping and indicators are emerging techniques that provide the opportunity to have collective community dialogues, to define the elements that comprise a healthy community, to translate community priorities into data that can be monitored over time, and to aggregate inexpensive, compelling, easy-to-use evidence for community advocacy. Strategies include:

- Develop and provide necessary data sets.
- Provide technical assistance on the technology and advocacy potential of maps and in support of local indicator projects.
- Establish standards and guidance for indicators and indicator reports to track improvements in inequities (i.e., the community characteristics and the health outcomes).
- Enhance state and local public health departments' ability to access electronic health records and data to facilitate timely public health surveillance, trend and outbreak detection, and geographical analysis to link environmental determinants to patterns of disease distribution.
- Link the mapping of medical conditions and community conditions to better assess their interplay and develop effective environmental solutions that reduce the incidence of these conditions (e.g., compare traffic injury data to neighborhoods or diabetes rates to supermarket locations).

Jacksonville, Florida Quality of Life Progress Report

In 1985, the Jacksonville Community Council Inc. (JCCI) developed the nation's first community-based quality-of-life indicators assessment. The assessment, published annually as the Quality of Life Progress Report, uses indicators to measure and monitor factors that encompass the social determinants of health in Jacksonville and surrounding communities in northeast Florida. In 2002, race relations and disparities in health and social circumstances based on race in Jacksonville were selected as a topic for deep community-led study. The resulting study, guided by community participation, documented that racial disparities were prevalent locally in six areas: education, income and employment, housing, health, criminal justice, and the political process. Following completion of the study, JCCI produced a report outlining 27 recommendations to improve race relations in Jacksonville and eliminate racial disparities.

One of the primary recommendations stated that JCCI should convene citizens to create and distribute an annual report card on race relations in Jacksonville, modeled after the Quality of Life Progress Report. In 2005, JCCI released the first Race Relations Progress Report measuring race-based disparities as well as perceptions of racism and discrimination in the community. The report guides policy decisions and community work and measures progress toward an inclusive community free of race-based disparities or discrimination. It has since become an annual report card and review of its findings has become institutionalized in local government. Some of the policy changes that have resulted from the Progress Report's findings include:

- Establishment of The Jacksonville Re-entry Center, a one-stop shop for ex-offenders looking for housing, employment, substance abuse treatment, legal assistance, and counseling.
- The Mayor embarked on a comprehensive literacy campaign.
- A Mayoral Proclamation and City Council Resolution supporting public policy that promotes equity and justice in Jacksonville.
- The City Council approved spending $900,000 to help supplement the JaxCare Program to reduce racial inequities.

S7 Provide technical assistance and tools to support community-level efforts to address determinants of health and reduce inequities.

- Provide access to tools and resources to assess and address the elements that can maximize health (e.g., indicators and report cards, maps, and community assessment tools).
- Provide access to high-quality, culturally appropriate technical assistance and training in planning, implementing, and evaluating.

Community planning using THRIVE

THRIVE (Tool for Health and Resilience in Vulnerable Environments) is a community resilience assessment tool that provides a framework for community members, coalitions, public health practitioners, and local decision makers to identify factors associated with poor health outcomes in communities of color, engage relevant stakeholders, and take action to remedy the disparities. Grounded in research, it has demonstrated utility in urban, rural, and suburban settings. Within months of piloting, several communities had initiated farmers' markets and youth programs.[65] One began to take health and safety considerations into account in planning decisions. At the community level, the THRIVE tool contributed to a broad vision about community health, confirmed the value of upstream approaches, challenged traditional thinking about health promotion, organized difficult concepts, enabled systematic planning, and proved to be a good tool for strategic planning at community and organizational levels.

For more information on THRIVE, visit: http://preventioninstitute.org/thrive/index.php.

APPENDIX A

Overarching Recommendations
Support local efforts through leadership, overarching policies, and through local, state, and national strategy

O1 Develop a national strategy to promote health equity across racial, ethnic, and socioeconomic lines, with specific attention to preventing injury and illness in the first place. A national strategy could provide an overall framework and direction and set a clear expectation that reducing health inequities is a national priority. Although this paper is about local efforts, there is a critical interplay of the local, state, and national and thus we identify some of the national steps that must be taken in support of local approaches. Components of a national strategy should include:

- Establishing high-level leadership at the White House and the department level to serve as a focal point for strategy on health equity and to ensure collaboration among government agencies.
- Building the capacity of federal, state, and local health agencies to lead health equity work.
- Expanding funding for community-based initiatives.
- Providing technical assistance and tools to support community-level efforts to address determinants of health, improve health care outcomes, and reduce disparities.
- Supporting the development of national, state, and local data systems to inform community efforts, foster accountability, and build a stronger understanding of what it takes to achieve health equity.

> **World Health Organization's Commission on Social Determinants of Health: Overarching Recommendations, 2008**[66]
>
> 1. Improve the conditions of daily life—the circumstances in which people are born, grow, live, work, and age.
> 2. Tackle the inequitable distribution of power, money, and resources—the structural drivers of those conditions of daily life—globally, nationally, and locally.
> 3. Measure the problem, evaluate action, expand the knowledge base, develop a workforce that is trained in the social determinants of health, and raise public awareness about the social determinants of health.

- Furthering research on and significantly expanding the amount and proportion of federal research dollars for population-based prevention and health equity, with an emphasis on translating the findings into targeted, community-specific strategies.
- Fostering new leadership to advance health equity work and ensure that attention to achieving health equity is embedded into the priorities, practices, and policies of government entities, private organizations, the health care system, and communities.

O2 Provide federal resources to support state and local community-based prevention strategies. Strategies for federal health agencies (such as Health and Human Services, the Centers for Disease Control and Prevention, Health Resources Services Administration, and the National Institutes of Health) include:

- Fund local public health agencies to craft local, flexibly designed community prevention strategies that are relevant to local conditions.

- Align existing strategies and policies with those of other federal agencies such as the Department of Education, Environmental Protection Agency, United States Department of Agriculture, Housing and Urban Development, and Department of Transportation so that states and local communities can leverage resources and efforts.
- Grant regulatory waivers to states seeking to create financial incentives for community-based prevention efforts that reduce medical care costs.
- Reimburse such strategies as fall-prevention for seniors, nurse home visitation for high risk infants, asthma environmental risk reduction initiatives, diabetes peer counseling, promotoras programs, and other proven and promising community-based prevention efforts must be reimbursed.

New York City Center for Economic Opportunity

The New York City Center for Economic Opportunity (CEO), established by Mayor Michael Bloomberg in December 2006, provides an innovative model for implementing, monitoring, and evaluating a successful urban anti-poverty agenda. Through its emphasis on strategies that achieve immediate results and longer-term investments focused on results-based policy and programmatic interventions, the CEO's early successes and promising initiatives include:

- Developing an alternative to the outdated 40-year old federal poverty measure that more accurately captures the number of people living in poverty. Congressman Jim McDermott (D-WA) and Senator Christopher Dodd (D-CT) have since introduced legislation to revise the federal poverty measure.
- Using pre-populated Earned Income Tax Credits (EITC) forms to help eligible low-income New Yorkers receive almost $14 million in EITC.
- Placing 2,166 low-income job seekers from high poverty areas in jobs in 2009.
- Providing financial and academic assistance to low-income students to attend City University of New York Accelerated Associate's Program increasing anticipated
- 2-year graduation rates from 12.5% to 30%.
- Providing a Child Care Tax Credit for low- to moderate-income working families that provided $30 million in assistance to over 50,000 eligible families in the first year alone.

Building on the local success of CEO, New York City has recently put forth a proposal for a Federal Urban Innovation Fund to be administered by the White House to help support a national urban poverty agenda by dissolving the existing government silos that have hampered success.

For more information about the Center for Economic Opportunity, visit: www.nyc.gov/ceo

03 Tackle the inequitable distribution of power, money, and resources—the structural drivers of the conditions of daily life that contribute to inequitable health and safety outcomes—and especially address race, racism, and discrimination in institutions and polices; racial and socioeconomic segregation; and socioeconomic conditions.
Poverty, racism, and lack of educational and economic opportunities are among the fundamental determinants of poor health, lack of safety, and health inequities. Strategies include:

- Assess institutional policies and practices for race, racism, and discrimination—including holding discussions about race and racism within institutions—and modify practices and policies accordingly.

APPENDIX A

- Conduct a comprehensive review of policies and practices that contribute to racial and socioeconomic segregation, delineate recommended policies to reverse segregation, and include attention to demonstrated promising strategies to reverse residential segregation.
- Improve socioeconomic conditions by 1) raising incomes of the poor, especially those with children (increase enrollment in income support programs; raise the state minimum wage; implement local living wage ordinances); 2) assisting poor people in accumulating assets (provide education and financial counseling to increase access to savings accounts and investment programs; expand home ownership and micro-enterprise opportunities); and 3) supporting job creation and workforce development (negotiate community benefits agreements; preserve industrial land for well-paid jobs; expand local green collar jobs; increase access to education, training, and career ladders; fund job readiness and skill-building programs).
- Reform criminal justice laws to address disproportionate incarceration rates for African Americans, Latinos, and low-income people such as by decriminalizing addiction and implementing community programs for drug offenders in lieu of prison; supporting mental health treatment for those in need, including those with Post Traumatic Stress Disorder; and supporting effective re-entry programs.

04 Improve access to quality education and improve educational outcomes.

Educational attainment is one of the strongest predictors of income, and there is a strong relationship between income and health.[67,68] Even independent from income, education is associated with improved health outcomes: each additional year in school correlates to increased life expectancy and better health.[69] Strategies include:

- Reform school funding to equalize access to quality education in K–12, including providing equal access to technology to develop job readiness for 21st century jobs.
- Invest in recruiting, training, and retaining teachers, particularly to work in disadvantaged schools, and create incentives for teachers to remain in these schools.
- Provide need-based supports to schools, students, and parents—including positive interventions for at-risk middle and high school students and creating greater support for low-income parents of color to participate in their child's education.

"It is not possible to eliminate health disparities without simultaneously reducing disparities in educational achievement. By bringing together programs to improve health and school achievement and by making reducing school dropout rates a public health, educational, and human rights priority, public health professionals have the opportunity to make a lasting contribution to promoting population health and social justice."
REFRAMING SCHOOL DROPOUT AS A PUBLIC HEALTH ISSUE, CDC ARTICLE, OCT. 2007

Library cards for all

A simple yet innovative change in practice resulted in more young people reading, engaging in meaningful opportunities, having a safe place to gather, and connecting with their community. In Salinas, California, the library and schools partnered to provide all students with library cards, free of charge and application-free. Further, the library eliminated fines and fees for the first year to enable students to learn about using the library. Since the change, the library has seen a significant increase in library usage by young people and their families. Moreover, the community feels the importance of libraries in their lives, a constituency for libraries has been built, and more young people and their families are reading and spending time together.

05 Invest in early childhood. During the first five years of life, every encounter a child has or lacks is formative. For healthy development, young children need a range of supports, social and emotional care, and nurturing.[70] Strategies include:

- Provide high quality and affordable child care and preschools; ensure equitable distribution of and access to preschools and provide subsidies.
- Invest in home visiting initiatives such as the Nurse Family Partnership.
- Invest in recruiting, training, and retaining child care providers.

Consistent investment in Nurse Family Partnership (NFP) initiatives

NFP is a child abuse prevention and mental health treatment program in which trained public health nurses make regular home visits to low-income, first-time mothers. Designed by Dr. David Olds of Colorado, the program reduces the child's risk for antisocial behavior by improving maternal and child health and reducing the risk of child abuse. Visits from nurses during pregnancy and through the first two years of a child's life help parents promote healthy emotional development, establish a positive relationship with their child, and build self-efficacy as an adult and parent.

The program has been successfully implemented in rural, urban, and various ethnic communities. It has reduced child abuse by 80% in the first two years of the child's life and had significant long-term benefits. Fifteen years after services ended, participants had one-third as many arrests and their children were half as likely to be delinquent compared to mothers and children without services. Women in the program also spent less time on welfare, smoked fewer cigarettes, and consumed less alcohol than families in control groups.[71]

States have utilized a number of mechanisms to secure ongoing funding: tobacco settlement dollars (Colorado, as defined by the Colorado Nurse Home Visitor Act), Medicaid Reimbursement and Block Grants (Louisiana), state appropriation (Oklahoma), and Temporary Assistance for Needy Families (Pennsylvania).

Conclusion: A Time of Opportunity

As interviews with public health leaders confirm, this is a time of opportunity. (For more detailed information, please see Appendix G: Opportunities.) Nationally, health and health care have emerged as major economic issues and as top priorities of the new Administration and Congress. There is growing understanding of the importance of healthy communities, the influence of their underlying health determinants, and of the role of culturally appropriate, family-centered primary care in accomplishing health equity.

Over the past several decades, there has been a general shift towards moving social programs from federal to state governments—a "devolution of authority." Although federal initiatives provided the catalyst for health disparities to emerge as a public health issue, states are now poised to build on this opportunity and take the lead in sponsoring policies and social programs that help reduce inequities. States are seen as a key place for health reform.[72] Numerous health departments are engaging in efforts to advance health equity in communities large and small, urban and rural.[73]

Focusing equity efforts at the state and local levels is promising because many of the social and economic health determinants can be acted upon at these levels. There is a strong national trend toward using community-level health indicators and indicator data to monitor change over time, increase accountability among policy makers, and engage communities in a dialogue about local priorities.

What's good for our health is good for our overall well-being. For example, the mounting concern over environmental degradation and the increased focus on prioritizing solutions, have introduced an opportunity to align issues of health and health equity with those of the environment and improve both simultaneously. Health is not only a major issue in and of itself, but it aligns with many of the other major concerns of our society.

In real estate, there are only three things that matter—location, location, location. Our conclusion as authors is that policy is vital and changing our organizational practices is critical; and it all must be done in service of people, where they live, work, play, socialize, and learn. In other words—community, community, community.

Acknowledgments

The authors would like to acknowledge the IOM Roundtable on Health Disparities for their commitment to addressing this important issue and for the opportunity to write this background paper. This report was produced in part with core support funding from Kaiser Permanente.

This paper builds on previous work of the Institute of Medicine, the authors, and many others who have contributed to better understanding and addressing health inequities. This paper synthesizes various bodies of work and input from many individuals. We apologize for any oversights and omissions, which are unintentional. We would like to thank the many people who provided input during the development of this paper. Their insight has been invaluable. They are:

Manal Aboelata, Prevention Institute
Karen Anderson, Institute of Medicine
Laurie Andress, Andress & Associates, LLC, Bridging the Health Gap
Judith Bell, PolicyLink
Georges Benjamin, American Public Health Association
Clement Bezold, Institute of Alternative Futures
Paula Braveman, University of California San Francisco
Colleen Campbell, Alameda County Department of Public Health
Joan Cleary, Blue Cross and Blue Shield of Minnesota Foundation
Ellen Clement, Washtenaw County Public Health Department
Sue Egerter, University of California San Francisco
Barbara Ferrer, Boston Public Health Commission
Jonathon Fielding, Los Angeles Public Health Department
Lark Galloway-Gilliam, Health Equity Coalition
Randall Henry, Veteran Affairs Greater Los Angeles Healthcare System
David Johnson, Minneapolis Department of Health and Family Support
Jim Krieger, Public Health - Seattle and King County
Julie Lee, Blue Cross and Blue Shield of Minnesota Foundation
Caya Lewis, Senate HELP Committee
Nicole Lurie, RAND
James Marks, Robert Wood Johnson Foundation
Steve Marks, Jewish Family and Children Services of Southern Arizona, Inc.
Leslie Mikkelsen, Prevention Institute
Edward O'Neil, University of California San Francisco
Bob Prentice, Bay Area Regional Health Inequities Initiative
Sara Rosenbaum, George Washington University

APPENDIX A

Anja Rudiger, National Economic and Social Rights Initiative/National Health Law Program
Linda Rudolf, Center for Chronic Disease Prevention and Health Promotion California Department of Public Health
Eduardo Sanchez, Blue Cross Blue Shield of Texas
Dean Schillinger, UCSF Center for Vulnerable Populations
Bruce Siegel, George Washington University School of Public Health and Health Services
Brian Smedley, The Joint Center for Political and Economic Studies
Hal Strelnick, Albert Einstein College of Medicine, Montefiore Medical Center
Mildred Thompson, PolicyLink
Robin Weinick, RAND
Winston Wong, Disparities Improvement and Quality Initiatives Kaiser Permanente
Michael Woods, Project Brotherhood
Ellen Wu, California Pan-Ethnic Health Network

The authors would also like to acknowledge their skilled editor, Anne Paniagua, who worked tirelessly to make the paper as clear and concise as possible and their graphic designer, Susan Lockwood of lockwood design, who worked quickly to turn around the final report.

Health Equity Toolkit Key Informants

Additionally, Prevention Institute conducted a set of key informant interviews with public health practitioners during Spring 2008, with funding from the Robert Wood Johnson Foundation, to inform the development of a Health Equity Toolkit. Prevention Institute synthesized interview findings and highlighted core themes from these interviews which are reflected in the challenges and opportunities sections of the paper and informed our thinking for the paper in general. Key informant interviews were conducted with:

Jayne Andreen, Alaska Department of Health and Social Services
Bobbi Berkowitz, University of Washington – School of Nursing, Department of Psychosocial & Community Health
James Bloyd, Cook County Department of Public Health
Andrew Goodman, New York City Department of Health and Mental Hygiene
Heidi Hataway, Alabama Department of Health
Richard Hofrichter, National Association of County and City Health Officials
Frances Kaplan, Arizona Department of Health Services
Vincent Lafronza, CommonHealth Action
Gwen Lipscomb, Alabama Department of Public Health, Minority Health Office
Zipatly Mendoza, Arizona Department of Health Services
Ngozi Oleru, Seattle & King County Department of Public Health
JT Petherick, Cherokee Nation
Paul Simon, Los Angeles County Department of Public Health
Adewale Troutman, Louisville Metro Public Health and Wellness, Center for Health Equity
Sandra Witt, Alameda County Public Health Department

Appendix A

Inequitable Rates of Morbidity & Mortality

Racial and ethnic minorities continue to experience higher rates of morbidity and mortality than non-minorities.[74] Low-income populations and people of color do not experience different injuries and illnesses than the rest of the population; they suffer from the same injuries and illnesses, only more frequently and severely. For example:

- Compared to Whites, American Indians and Alaska Natives are 2.3 times more likely to have diagnosed diabetes, African Americans are 2.2 times more likely, and Latinos are 1.6 times more likely.[75]
- Among African Americans between the ages of 10 and 24, homicide is the leading cause of death. In the same age range, homicide is the second leading cause of death for Hispanics, and the third leading cause of death for American Indians, Alaska Natives, and Asian/Pacific Islanders.[76] Homicide rates among non-Hispanic, African American males 10 to 24 years of age (58.3 per 100,000) exceed those of Hispanic males (20.9 per 100,000) and non-Hispanic, White males in the same age group (3.3 per 100,000).[77]
- Native Americans have a motor vehicle death rate that is more than 1.5 times greater than Whites, Latinos, Asian/Pacific Islanders, and African Americans.[78,79]
- Poverty is associated with risk factors for chronic health conditions, and low-income adults report multiple serious health conditions more often than those with higher incomes.[80]
- The average annual incidence of end-stage kidney disease in minority zip codes was nearly twice as high as in non-minority zip codes.[81]
- Premature death rates from cardiovascular disease (i.e., between the ages of 5 and 64) were substantially higher in minority zip codes than in non-minority zip codes.[82]
- Education correlates strongly with health. Among adults over age 25, 5.8% of college graduates, 11% of those with some college, 13.9% of high school graduates, and 25.7% of those with less than a high school education report being in poor or fair health.[83]

Appendix B

Definitions of Health Disparities and Health Inequities

The National Institutes of Health defines *health disparities* as "differences in the incidence, prevalence, mortality, and burden of diseases and other adverse health conditions that exist among specific population groups in the United States."[84]

Health inequities are "differences in health which are not only unnecessary and avoidable but, in addition, are considered unfair and unjust."[85]

Thus, equity and inequity are based on core American values of fairness and justice whereas "disparity" is a narrow descriptive term that refers to measurable differences but does not imply whether this disparity arises from an unjust root cause.

For the purposes of this paper, the term "inequity" is used when the referenced differences in health outcomes have been produced by historic and systemic social injustices, or the unintended or indirect consequences of social policies.

Appendix C

The Economics of Prevention—Reducing Health Care Costs through Prevention

Currently, health care spending is growing at an unsustainable rate[86] (see Figure 1) driven by both rising costs and a growing burden of disease. In addition to straining public resources, the costs are bankrupting families and small businesses, and putting corporations and industry at a competitive disadvantage. How do we remedy this? The long-term solution must involve both cost containment and reduced demand for services. Currently, our nation spends over two trillion dollars each year on health expenditures and approximately 96% of this is expended on medical services—treatment after the onset of illnesses and injuries.[87] Nevertheless, access to health care only accounts for 10% of the variation in morbidity and mortality; other factors that determine health include environments and behaviors.[88]

A vital strategy for creating a sustainable health care system is to improve health status through prevention-reducing demand not by denying service but by reducing the need for service. A review of the literature[89] shows the following:

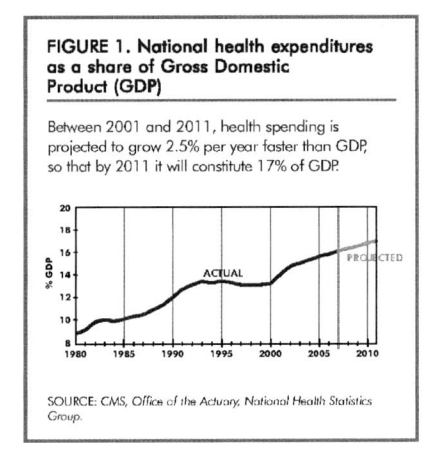

FIGURE 1. National health expenditures as a share of Gross Domestic Product (GDP)

Between 2001 and 2011, health spending is projected to grow 2.5% per year faster than GDP, so that by 2011 it will constitute 17% of GDP.

SOURCE: CMS, Office of the Actuary, National Health Statistics Group.

1. A majority of the most costly health conditions are preventable.
2. Health-related resources are not invested in the areas that most influence health.
3. A 5% reduction in preventable illnesses and injuries could lead to substantial savings.
4. Savings have been demonstrated and forecasted for specific prevention initiatives.
5. Prevention has the potential to reduce end-of-life care costs.
6. Savings from prevention accrue beyond the health care sector.
7. Prevention could help improve productivity and competitiveness.
8. New economic models predict potential cost savings from prevention.

Further, an economic analysis revealed that investing even the modest amount of $10 per person in community level initiatives aimed at reducing tobacco consumption, improving nutrition, and increasing physical activity results in a return on investment within two years and an estimated annual savings of over $15 billion nationally within five years.[90] Each year thereafter, the 5 to 1 return on investment is projected to continue. The savings from an investment in prevention in disenfranchised communities should be even greater because they experience the greatest burden of ill health. In addition to this chronic disease analysis, studies reveal that other health-related investments also yield a significant return. For instance, $1 invested in breastfeeding support by employers results in $3 in reduced absenteeism and health care costs for mothers and babies and improved productivity; $1 invested in lead abatement in public housing returns $2 in reduced medical and special education costs and increased productivity; and $1 invested in workplace safety measures returns $4 to $6 in reduced illnesses, injuries, and fatalities.[91,92]

Appendix D

Reasons why addressing access to and quality of health care alone will not significantly reduce inequities

1. *Health care is not the primary determinant of health.* Of the 30-year increase in life expectancy since the turn of the century, only about five years of this increase are attributed to medical care interventions.[93] Even in countries with universal access to care, people with lower socioeconomic status have poorer health outcomes.[94]

2. *Health care treats one person at a time.* By focusing on the individual and specific illnesses as they arise, medical treatment does not reduce the incidence or severity of disease among groups of people because others become afflicted even as others are cured.[95]

3. *Health intervention often comes late.* Medical care and intervention play important restorative or ameliorating roles after disease occurs. Further many of today's most common chronic health conditions, such as heart disease, diabetes, asthma, and HIV/AIDS, are never cured. It is extremely important to prevent them from occurring in the first place and, when they occur, their ongoing prognosis will depend on a number of factors in addition to medical care.

Appendix E

A Health Equity Framework: Taking Two Steps Back to the Determinants of Health

The frequency and severity of injury and illness are not inevitable. The Two Steps Back framework was developed as a tool for analyzing the underlying causes of illness and injury and health inequities and identifying the key opportunities for intervention and prevention. Two Steps Back presents a systematic way of looking at needed medical services and then traveling back to the exposures and behaviors that affect illness and injury and then back to the underlying community conditions that shape patterns of exposure and behavior.

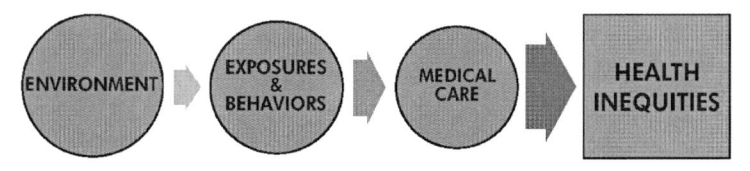

ENVIRONMENT → EXPOSURES & BEHAVIORS → MEDICAL CARE → HEALTH INEQUITIES

STARTING WITH MEDICAL CARE

Medical care aims to improve health outcomes by focusing on identifying and treating specific medical conditions (e.g., heart disease, diabetes and infections) with medical services. High-quality medical care can prevent the onset of some medical conditions, diagnose problems early, reduce the severity of symptoms, and slow the progression of secondary conditions. The Institute of Medicine's *Unequal Treatment: Confronting Racial and Ethnic Disparities in Health Care* identified three primary ways to intervene to reduce health inequities through medical care:[96]

- **Increase access to care:** Within our current system, lack of insurance and under-insurance, major barriers to accessing medical care, are not borne equally across racial and ethnic lines.
- **Improve quality of care (diagnosis and treatment):** *Unequal Treatment* documents that "evidence of racial and ethnic disparities in healthcare is, with few exceptions, remarkably consistent across a range of illnesses and healthcare services." *Unequal Treatment* reveals that differences in diagnosis, quality of care, and treatment methods lead to consistently poorer health outcomes among people of color.
- **Implement culturally and linguistically appropriate care:** A culturally competent system of care is measured both by achieving the desired health outcome and patient satisfaction with medical encounters.[97]

TAKING A STEP BACK:
From Medical Care to Exposures and Behaviors

Medical care alone cannot eliminate health disparities. The first step back is from medical care to exposures and behaviors. Limiting unhealthy exposures and behaviors enhances health and reduces the likelihood and severity of disease. Through an analysis of the factors contributing to medical conditions that cause people to seek care, researchers have identified a set of nine behaviors and exposures strongly linked to the major causes of death: tobacco, diet and activity patterns, alcohol, microbial agents, toxic agents, firearms, sexual behavior, motor vehicles, and inappropriate drug use.[98] These behaviors and exposures are linked to multiple medical diagnoses sand addressing them can improve health broadly. For example, tobacco is associated with a number of health problems including

APPENDIX A

lung cancer, asthma, emphysema, and heart disease. Diet and activity patterns are associated with cardiovascular and heart disease, certain cancers, and diabetes, among other illnesses.

As a result, reducing exposures and unhealthy behaviors decreases the risk of multiple injuries and illnesses. It is also important to include analysis of exposure to the stressors of poverty, racism, lack of opportunity, etc. Exposure to these stressors affects low-income communities and people of color disproportionately, and similar to the nine listed above are contributing factors in multiple health conditions and opportunities for intervention.

THE SECOND STEP BACK:
From Exposures and Behaviors to the Environment

Exposures and behaviors are determined or shaped by the environments in which they are present, defined as anything external to individuals and shared by members of a community. Exposures, of course, are shaped by what in the environment one is exposed to, and behaviors are shaped (encouraged or discouraged) by what is available in communities and the norms that communities help shape. Taking the second step back from exposures and behaviors to the environment, presents a tremendous opportunity to reduce health inequities by preventing illness and injury *before* their onset. The environment includes root factors (e.g., poverty, racism, and other forms of oppression), institutions, and community factors. THRIVE (Tool for Health and Resilience in Vulnerable Environments), a research-based framework created by Prevention Institute, offers a way to understand the community factors.[99] THRIVE includes 13 community health factors grouped into three clusters: people, place, and equitable opportunity. Similar work by other researchers confirms this overall approach. For example, in 2002 PolicyLink published very similar findings and factors in the report, *Reducing Health Disparities Through a Focus on Communities*.[100]

The 13 community factors are organized into 3 interrelated clusters: equitable opportunity, people, and place (see Table 1: *Community Factors Affecting Health, Safety, and Mental Health*) and either directly influence health and safety outcomes via exposures (e.g., air, water, soil quality; stressors) or indirectly via behaviors that in turn affect health and safety outcomes (e.g., the availability of healthy food affects nutrition). In addition, the environment also influences people's opportunity to access quality medical services, and these are included as a 4th cluster. The clusters are described here:

EQUITABLE OPPORTUNITY: This cluster refers to the level and equitable distribution of opportunity and resources. Root factors, including poverty, racism, and lack of educational and economic opportunities are among the fundamental determinants of poor health, lack of safety, and health inequities. They each contribute to chronic stress and can build upon one another to create a weathering effect, whereby health greatly reflects cumulative experience rather than chronological or developmental age.[101] Chronic stress increases risk for coronary artery disease, stroke, cognitive impairment, substance abuse, anxiety, depression, mood disorders, and accelerated aging and cancer.[102] Further, economic and racial segregation is one of the most powerful forces shaping health in the US. The availability of jobs with living wages, absence of discrimination and racism, and quality education all affect health and safety.[103,104] This segregation is not inevitable; it has been established and maintained through government policy and investment and the practices of institutions and organizations.[105] Examples include redlining (wherein low-income neighborhoods and neighborhoods with primarily people of color are identified for discriminatory investment by banks and other lenders, historically by drawing a red line on a map); discriminatory application of GI Bill housing benefits; unequal investment in schools and transportation (leaving low-income communities at an educational and geographic disadvantage, which restricts social and economic mobility and development leading to further concentration of poverty); and judicial rulings such as the Supreme Court's recent ruling (Parents Involved in Community Schools v. Seattle School District) that reverses much of Brown v. Board of Education, which ruled that separate was not equal.)

PEOPLE: This cluster refers to the relationships between people, the level of engagement, and norms, all of which influence health and safety outcomes. For instance, strong social networks and connections correspond with significant increases in physical and mental health, academic achievement, and local economic development, as well as lower rates of homicide, suicide, and alcohol and drug abuse;[106,107] children have been found to be mentally and physically healthier in neighborhoods where adults talk to each other.[108] Social connections also contribute to a community's willingness to take action for the common good which is associated with lower rates of violence,[109] and improved food access.[110]

PLACE: This cluster refers to the physical environment in which people live, work, play, and go to school. Decisions about place have multiple direct and indirect effects on health and safety. For example, physical activity levels are influenced by conditions such as enjoyable scenery,[111] the proximity of recreational facilities, street and neighborhood design,[112] and transportation design;[113] each supermarket in an African American census tract, fruit and vegetable intake has been show to increase by 32%;[114] and the presence of alcohol distributors in a community is correlated with per capita consumption.[115]

HEALTH CARE SERVICES: Over the course of our lives we also all want and need health care, including good medical, mental health, and dental services. As a starting point, people need to be able to obtain quality medical and dental care, which means people need adequate and affordable health insurance. To help maintain health, people need preventive care and chronic disease management. In crisis situations, we need reliable, immediate, and qualified emergency medical responses. When we suffer from acute or chronic conditions, we hope for quality medical care to treat or cure our conditions, or help us manage them. For all of these services, culturally and linguistically appropriate patient care is critical for communicating with patients and addressing health concerns within the cultural context of the patient.

Appendix F

The Role of Health Care Providers in Reducing Intimate Partner Violence (IPV)

Health care providers are at the intersection of health, violence, and community. They can use their tremendous influence and credibility to help tip the balance and more systematically prevent IPV.

Clinical Practice

As sources of credibility and regular interaction, health care providers play an important role in the primary prevention of IPV.[116,117] Major clinical practices that support IPV prevention include engaging women in an empowering way,[118] promoting healthy relationships and sexuality, and dialoguing with parents and parents-to-be. Examples include:[119-122]

- Examining own personal attitudes that may serve to contribute to prevalent social norms that allow for abuse (i.e., blaming the victim). "Why won't she leave?" needs to be replaced with "What will make him stop?"[123-125]
- Using a longitudinal, age-specific approach to engage women and girls developmentally to help reinforce messages throughout a woman's life stages.[126]
- Engaging patients as active participants during regular examinations through dialogue and a restructuring of the examination room.
- Dialoguing with parents and parents-to-be, such as encouraging parents to promote flexible sex role socialization of their children by broadening the views of parents regarding behaviors considered "natural" for either gender.[127,128]
- Promoting and modeling healthy relationships.

Organizational Practices

Since institutions shape and reinforce norms, it is critical that healthcare settings and professional associations establish and promulgate regulations, practices, and cultures that contribute to IPV reduction. Areas of focus include training and policies, as well as reflecting an egalitarian culture and intolerance of violence and patriarchy. Examples include:

- Establish work place policies that are in alignment with ending IPV (e.g., anti-harassment policies and training on and modeling egalitarian relationships and appropriate ways of handling conflict.)
- Establish policies to enable healthcare practitioners to teach about IPV in the community.
- Provide information and resources to patients, such as in waiting rooms and clinics, about healthy relationships and to raise clients' consciousness of sexist attitudes in the media that promote sex and violence.[129-131]
- Encourage ongoing professional development and continuing education on preventing IPV that includes promoting healthy relationships and sexuality.

Spokesperson/Advocate

Health care institutions and providers can be powerful advocates for prevention. Providers must speak up in their clinical practices, in their organizations and associations, and broadly to the public, the media, and policymakers. By speaking up in public meetings, serving as experts to the media and testifying to legislators, health care providers can shape issues, influence the debate, and challenge public and political discourse. Examples include:

- Advocating for decreases in the portrayal of violence in the media,
- Supporting state and national legislative efforts, and
- Petitioning for legal remedies designed to protect women.[132]

Appendix G

Opportunities

Building on interviews with local health officers conducted to inform the development of a Health Equity Toolkit funded by the Robert Wood Johnson Foundation as part of the project *Advancing Public Health Advocacy to Eliminate Health Disparities*, we have identified opportunities to advance health equity work.

1. The time has come for health reform

Nationally, health and health care have emerged as major economic issues and as top priorities of the new Administration and Congress. When we consider health reform, it is critical that we highlight underlying determinants of health. We have made the case for the economics of community-oriented prevention.[133,134] With a growing awareness of community conditions for health, of tools that help make the case for addressing the underlying causes of health inequities (e.g., the PBS documentary series, *Unnatural Causes: Is Inequality Making Us Sick?*), and of the role of culturally appropriate, family-centered primary care, the pieces are in place to inform a more equitable, health-producing health system that is sustainable for all. To reduce inequities in health and safety, health reform will need to draw upon community-level prevention to decrease the number of people getting sick and injured; reimburse for medical services, including preventive medical services that are delivered in communities; and assure that system redesign enables the delivery of high-quality, culturally appropriate health care services for all.

2. It makes a lot of sense to focus at the state and local levels to address inequities

Over the past several decades, there has been a general shift towards moving social programs from federal to state governments—a "devolution of authority." Although federal initiatives provided the catalyst for health disparities to emerge as a public health issue, states are now poised to build on this opportunity and take the lead in sponsoring social programs that help reduce inequities. States are seen as a key place for health reform.[135] Numerous health departments are engaging in efforts to advance health equity in communities large and small, urban and rural.[136] In some cases, departments are deeply engaged in equity-focused work and are creating organizational structures and processes to focus specifically on health equity. In other cases, departments are engaged in supportive ways, sharing resources and information with community-based organizations that are providing more of the leadership and energy behind equity efforts. Many health departments are in an exploratory phase, examining internal interest and opportunities for addressing health equity.

Focusing equity efforts at the state and local levels is promising because many of the social and economic health determinants can be acted upon at these levels. For example, a local health department seeking to ensure quality affordable housing can work with the local community development and housing agency to discuss proposed projects, provide data about their potential health impacts, and work with local residents to explore their needs and concerns. Commitment and optimism about health equity becoming a centerpiece of the public heath agenda remains high within health departments as they strive to make the internal and external changes neces-

APPENDIX A

sary to take on an equity-related focus. There remains a need to further coalesce and project a stronger community voice, though partnerships with community organizations and policy makers have proven successful.[137]

3. Our ability to map, measure and track is improving significantly

Emerging technologies, coupled with new and expanding sources of data, are providing significant support in reducing health inequities. For instance, community-based organizations and public agencies are increasingly using maps to support social and economic change on a community level. Mapping is a powerful tool in two ways: (1) it makes patterns based on place much easier to identify and analyze and (2) it provides a visual way of communicating those patterns to a broad audience, quickly and dramatically.[138] Projects such as Healthy City in Los Angeles allow users with minimal technical skill to create a variety of maps that highlight patterns of community resources, community conditions (e.g., income level or air quality), and health and social outcomes (e.g., disease rates or high school graduation rates). These maps provide stark illustration of community issues and can be used as the focus of community decision making and organizing and as important evidence during advocacy campaigns.

There is a strong national trend toward using community-level health indicators and indicator data to monitor change over time, increase accountability among policy makers, and engage communities in a dialog about local priorities. This movement is being supported by national institutions and resources, such as the Community Health Status Indicators Project, and implemented at regional and local levels. Well-selected community health indicators provide comparative data over time and are a step toward ensuring that actions are aligned with health interests, that the social determinants of health are monitored and acted upon, and that there is accountability for improving community conditions. The process of selecting indicators and collecting data—in essence selecting what will be measured—is in itself valuable as a venue for developing community capacity, building partnerships, and engaging community members, along with representatives from the public and private sectors, in identifying, prioritizing, and setting benchmarks related to health and well-being. Prevention Institute conducted a review of more than 90 indicator reports and report cards for the study *Good Health Counts: A 21st Century Approach to Community Health*.[139] This review revealed that success was achieved through both a carefully developed set of indicators that reflect the determinants of health within the community and a well-orchestrated, transparent process.

Movement toward the use of electronic medical records and shared data among hospitals also holds promise for examining differences in access and equity in hospitals and clinics. As hospitals and clinics move toward electronic systems, the capacity to analyze differences by race and ethnicity increases as does the potential to address issues of high rates of missing race/ethnicity data—a key parameter for establishing the presence of disparities. Taking appropriate steps to protect privacy, we can link this data to GIS mapping to yield powerful information about the impact of community environment on health.

4. What's good for our natural environment is good for our health

The mounting concern over environmental degradation and the increased focus on prioritizing solutions, have introduced an opportunity to align issues of health and health equity with those of the environment and improve both simultaneously. For instance, greenhouse gas emissions are bad for the environment generally, accelerate climate change, and also have direct repercussion on health (e.g., asthma rates). In our efforts to solve these challenges, we can build powerful partnerships and address health issues that might otherwise be diminished. Strategically improving the physical environment could reduce the number of people getting sick and injured in the first place as well as the severity of those diseases. In effect this could reduce the demand for medical services and the burden on the health care system. It could potentially increase the accessibility and affordability of quality health care and reduce the ecological footprint of our health care institutions.

Shifting towards a more sustainable food system and altering our transportation systems to support public transportation, walking, and biking, are among the initiatives that hold multiple environmental and health benefits by virtue of reducing greenhouse gases and our dependence on fossil fuels while improving air quality and increasing physical activity. There is potential to engage in strategies that simultaneously improve environmental conditions and support the health of vulnerable populations. Policies and practices are needed to improve the environmental and health conditions of communities—including ensuring clean air and water; preserving agricultural lands; reducing exposure to toxins; and providing economic opportunity, quality housing, and safe streets. However, such work must be done cautiously. For instance, rises in gas prices without simultaneous expansion of public transportation may have a positive impact in terms of greenhouse gases but can have disastrous effects on low-income people who live in communities that have been designed around automobile travel and where access to employment and resources such as healthy food are contingent on driving. As another example, popular "cap and trade" policies need to be implemented with safeguards against high polluters moving into communities with limited political capital to oppose such moves.

5. Internal organizational diversity helps to move along an equity-focused health agenda

Achieving greater diversity within the health professions has been identified as a key strategy for ensuring a culturally competent workforce. Greater diversity across all levels of an organization can seed new and creative strategies for tackling health inequities. A number of health organizations are currently at the forefront of efforts to address health equity, and all these organizations—including health departments, health care organizations, and community-based organizations—have the opportunity to increase the diversity of their staffs. Diversity goes beyond racial and ethnic diversity to include factors such as age, gender, socioeconomic status, sexual preference, and professional skills. Ways to build and sustain diverse leadership include proactive efforts to recruit, hire, train, and retain staff that will contribute to diversity.[140] Many organizations explicitly looking to address health equity have found that workforce development strategies can build the capacities of current staff and attract skilled and committed individuals to partake in the mission to achieve health equity. Organizations, as a result, seed new and creative ideas for tackling health inequities.

APPENDIX A

Endnotes

1. Life and Death From Unnatural Causes: Health & Social Inequity in Alameda County. Alameda County Public Health Department September 2008.

2. Geronimus AT. Understanding and eliminating racial inequalities in women's health in the United States: the role of the weathering conceptual framework. *J Am Med Womens Assoc.* 2001;56:133-6, 149-50.

3. U.S. Department of Health and Human Services. (1999). *Mental Health: A report of the Surgeon General.* Rockville, MD. Supplement: Mental Health: Culture, Race, And Ethnicity

4. Decades of Work to Reduce Disparities in Health Care Produce Limited Success. Rebecca Voelker. *JAMA.* 2008;299(12):1411-1413

5. House J.S., & Williams D.R. (2000). Understanding and reducing socioeconomic and racial/ethnic disparities in health. In B. Smedley, & S. Syme (Eds.), *Promoting health: intervention strategies from social and behavioral research.* Washington, D.C.: National Academy Press.

6. The World health report 2000: health systems : improving performance. Geneva, Switzerland: World Health Organization.

7. OECD Health Data 2007.

8. Schoen C, Osborn R, How S, Doty M, Peugh J. In Chronic Condition: Experiences of Patients with Complex Health Care Needs, In Eight Countries, 2008. *Health Affairs.* Web Exclusive. November 2008.

9. Nursing Shortage Fact Sheet, American Association of Colleges of Nursing, Updated April 2009. Retrieved at www.aacn.nche.edu/Media/FactSheets/NursingShortage.htm. Accessed April 15, 2009.

10. Kenneth E. Thorpe, David H. Howard and Katya Galactionova. Differences In Disease Prevalence As A Source Of The U.S.-European Health Care Spending Gap. *Health Affairs,* 26, no. 6 (2007): w678-w686

11. Thorpe K, Factors accounting for the rise in health care spending in the United States: the role of rising disease prevalence and treatment intensity. *Public Health.* 2006 Nov;120(11):1002-7. Epub 2006 Oct 9

12. Kenneth Thorpe et al, The Rising Prevalence of Treated Disease: Effects on private Health Insurance Spending. *Health Affairs.* Volume 24, Supplement 1. 23 June 2005

13. Prevention for a Healthier America: Investments in Disease Prevention Yield Significant Savings, Stronger Communities. Trust for America's Health, Prevention Institute, Urban Institute. 2008.

14. Adler NE, Newman K. Socioeconomic disparities in health: pathways and policies. *Health Affairs.* 2002; 21(2): 60-76.

15. Poverty and Race Research Action Council analysis of U.S. Census Bureau data, with the assistance of Nancy A. Denton and Bridget J. Anderson, 2005.

16. Smedley B, Jeffries M, Adelman L, Cheng J. Race, Racial Inequity and Health Inequities: Separating Myth from Fact. 2008. Available at: www.unnaturalcauses.org/assets/uploads/file/Race_Racial_Inequality_Health.pdf

17. Morland K, Wing S, Diez Roux A, Poole C. Neighborhood characteristics associated with the location of food stores and food service places. *American Journal of Preventive Medicine.* 2002; 22:23-9.

18. National Highway Traffic Safety Administration. (2004, June). Sixth report to Congress, fourth report to the president: The national initiative for increasing safety belt use. Washington, DC: Author.

19. Mokdad AH, Marks JS, Stroup DF, Gerberding JL. Actual causes of death in the United States, 2000. JAMA. 2004;291:1238-1245.

20. Davis R, Cook D, Cohen L. A community resilience approach to reducing ethnic and racial disparities in health. Am J Public Health. 2005;95:2168-73

21. Prevention Institute. Health Equity Toolkit Key Informants Interview Synthesis document. 2008. Unpublished.

22. Prevention Institute. Health Equity Toolkit Key Informants Interview Synthesis document. 2008. Unpublished.

23. Siegel B, Bretsch J, Sears V, Regenstein M, Wilson M. Assumed Equity: Early Observations from the First Hospital Disparities Collaborative. Journal for Healthcare Quality 2007; Vol. 29, No. 5, pp 11-15.

24. U.S. Census Bureau. State & County QuickFacts. Richmond, California. Available at: http://quickfacts.census.gov/qfd/states/06/0660620.html Accessed on April 3, 2009.

25. Active Living Research. Robert Wood Johnson Foundation. Investigating policies and environments to support active communities. Active Living Research. Available at: www.activelivingresearch.org/files/briefing0305.pdf. Published March 2005. Accessed 15 April 2009.

26. Larson N, Story M, Nelson M. Neighborhood Environments Disparities in Access to Healthy Foods in the U.S. American Journal of Preventive Medicine 2009; 36(1): 74-81.

27. Sloane DC, Diamant AL, Lewis LB, et al. (2003). Improving the nutritional resource environment for healthy living through community-based participatory research. Journal of General Internal Medicine, 18, 568-575.

28. Pennsylvania Fresh Food Financing Initiative. Providing Healthy Food Choices to Pennsylvania's Communities. www.thefoodtrust.org/pdf/2009FFFI.pdf Accessed on May 1, 2009.

29. M. Reeves, A. Katten, and M. Guzman, Pesticide Action Network and Californians for Pesticide Reform, "Fields of poison 2002: California farm workers and pesticides," 2002, Available at: www.panna.org/resources/gpc/gpc_200304.13.1.07.dv.html Accessed September 11, 2007.

30. Weiss, Billie. An Assessment of Youth Violence Prevention Activities in USA Cities. Urban Networks to Increase Thriving Youth (UNITY) through Violence Prevention. Southern California Injury Prevention Research Center UCLA School of Public Health. June 2008.

31. CeaseFire is an evidence-based public health approach to reducing violence, www.ceasefirechicago.org/ Accessed April 15, 2009.

32. Family Violence Prevention Fund. The Facts on Health Care and Domestic Violence. http://endabuse.org/userfiles/file/Children_and_Families/HealthCare.pdf accessed on 4/11/09

33. Family Violence Prevention Fund. The Facts on Immigrant Women and Domestic Violence. http://endabuse.org/userfiles/file/Children_and_Families/Immigrant.pdf Accessed 4/11/09

34. City of Minneapolis, BLUEPRINT FOR ACTION: Quarterly Report. October –December 2008 February 2009. Available at: www.ci.minneapolis.mn.us/dhfs/YVP-Quarterly-Report-Fourth-Quarter-2008.pdf. Accessed May 1, 2009.

35. City of Minneapolis, BLUEPRINT FOR ACTION: Quarterly Report. October –December 2008 February 2009. Available at: www.ci.minneapolis.mn.us/dhfs/YVP-Quarterly-Report-Fourth-Quarter-2008.pdf. Accessed May 1, 2009.

36. Stern MJ, Seifert SC. Working Paper #13- Cultural participation and communities: The role of individual and neighborhood effects. Social Impact of the Arts Project, University of Pennsylvania: 2000.

37. Brice Heath, S., Soep, E. & Roach, A. (1998). Living the Arts Through Language and Learning: A Report on Community-based Youth Organizations. In Americans for the Arts MONOGRAPHS, V2(7).

APPENDIX A

38. Catterall, J.S. Involvement in the Arts and Success in Secondary School. In *Americans for the Arts MONOGRAPHS*, V1(10).

39. Smedley B, Stith A, Nelson A eds., *Unequal Treatment: Confronting Racial and Ethnic Disparities in Health Care*. Washington,D.C.:The National Academies Press; 2003: 5

40. Smedley B, Stith A, Nelson A eds., *Unequal Treatment: Confronting Racial and Ethnic Disparities in Health Care*. Washington,D.C.:The National Academies Press; 2003: 5.

41. Smedley B. Moving Beyond Access: Achieving Equity In State Health Care Reform. *Health Affairs*, March/April 2008. Vol 27, No. 2, pp 447-455.

42. Smedley B, Alvarez B., Panares R, Fish-Parcham C, Adland S. Identifying and Evaluating Equity Provisions in State Health Care Reform. April 2008. Available at: www.commonwealthfund.org.

43. California Pan-Ethnic Health Network. A Blueprint for Success: Bringing Language Access to Millions of Californians. Available at: www.cpehn.org/pdfs/Sb853briefScreen.pdf. Accessed on April 3, 2009.

44. Trivedi A, Gibbs B, Nsiah-Jefferson L, Ayanian JZ, Prothrom-Stith D. Creating A State Minority Health Policy Report Card. *Health Affairs* March/April 2005. Vol 24, no. 2; pp388-396.

45. Siegel B, Bretsch J, Sears V, Regenstein M, Wilson M. Assumed Equity: Early Observations from the First Hospital Disparities Collaborative. *Journal for Healthcare Quality* 2007; Vol. 29, No. 5, pp 11-15.

46. Findings from UCSF IDEALL Study: How Can Public Health Systems Best Support People with Diabetes? 2009.

47. Effects of Self-Management Support on Structure, Process and Outcomes Among Vulnerable Patients with Diabetes: A 3-Arm Practical Clinical Trial. *Diabetes Care*. 2009; 32(4):559-566.

48. Handley, M., Shumway, M., & Schillinger D. Cost-Effectiveness of Automates Telephone Self-Management Support with Nurse Care Management Among Patients with Diabetes. *Annals of Family Medicine*. 2008; 6(5): 1-7.

49. Smedley B. Moving Beyond Access: Achieving Equity In State Health Care Reform. *Health Affairs*, March/April 2008. Vol 27, No. 2, pp 447-455.

50. Brennan Ramirez LK, Baker EA, Metzler M. Promoting Health Equity: A Resource to Help Communities Address Social Determinants of Health. Atlanta: US Department of Health and Human Services, Center for Disease Control and Prevention. 2008.

51. Russell S, Senior care innovator retiring: On Lok's alternative to nursing homes got its start in Chinatown, September 21, 2004. San Francisco Chronicle., B-1. Accessed on April 23, 2009 at www.sfgate.com/cgi-bin/article.cgi?file=/chronicle/archive/2004/09/21/BAGI48SA051.DTL. Accessed May 1, 2009.

52. Beal AC, Doty MM, Hernandez SE, Shea KK, Davis K, Closing the Divide: How Medical Homes Promote Equity in Health Care: Results From The Commonwealth Fund 2006 Health Care Quality Survey, The Commonwealth Fund, June 2007.

53. Smedley B. Moving Beyond Access: Achieving Equity In State Health Care Reform. *Health Affairs*, March/April 2008. Vol 27, No. 2, pp 447-455.

54. Smedley B. Moving Beyond Access: Achieving Equity In State Health Care Reform. *Health Affairs*, March/April 2008. Vol 27, No. 2, pp 447-455.

55. Smedley B, Stith A, Nelson A eds., *Unequal Treatment: Confronting Racial and Ethnic Disparities in Health Care*. Washington,D.C.:The National Academies Press; 2003: 5.

56. Smedley B. Moving Beyond Access: Achieving Equity In State Health Care Reform. *Health Affairs*, March/April 2008. Vol 27, No. 2, pp 447-455

57. Smedley B. Moving Beyond Access: Achieving Equity In State Health Care Reform. *Health Affairs*, March/April 2008. Vol 27, No. 2, pp 447-455

58. State of California, Department of Finance, 2000-2005. Sacramento, CA July 2007

59. Journal of the American academy of nurse practitioners, volume 21, issue 2, pages 116-122. published online: 2/12/09

60. Minneapolis Department of Health and Family Support, Program Description: Seen on da Streets.

61. Boston Public Health Commission, Mayor's Task Force Blueprint A plan to eliminate racial and ethnic disparities in health. June 2005. Available at: www.bphc.org/programs/healthequitysocialjustice/tools andreports/Forms%20%20Documents/Center%20Reports%20and%20Tools/BPHCOHEBlueprint.pdf on April 15, 2009. Accessed on April 3, 2009.

62. Boston Public Health Commission. Boston works to end racial and ethnic disparities in health Year One Report. Available at: www.bphc.org/programs/healthequitysocialjustice/toolsandreports/Forms%20%20 Documents/Center%20Reports%20and%20Tools/BPHCOHEdisp_year1report.pdf pg. 38 Accessed on April 15, 2009.

63. Prevention Institute. Health Equity Toolkit Key Informants Interview Synthesis document. 2008. Unpublished.

64. Smedley B., Alvarez B., Pañares R., Fish-Parcham C., Adland S., April 2008. Identifying and Evaluating Equity Provisions in State Health Care Reform. The Commonwealth Fund, pub. no. 1124.

65. Davis R, Cook C, Cohen L. A Community Resilience Approach to Reducing Ethnic and Racial Disparities in Health, *The American Journal of Public Health*. December 2005 (Vol. 95, No. 12).

66. World Health Organization Commission on Social Determinants of Health, 2008. Closing the Gap in a Generation: Health Equity through Action on the Social Determinants of Health.

67. Freudenber N, Rugis J. Reframing School Dropout as a Public Health Issue. Preventing Chronic Disease. Center for Disease Control and Prevention. 2007;4(4): 1-11. Available at: www.cdc.gov/pcd/issues/ 2007/oct/07_0063.htm. Accessed March 2008.

68. Ross CE, and Mirowsky J. Refining the Association between Education and Health: The Effects of Quantity, Credential, and Selectivity. *Demography*. 1999;36(4): 445-460.

69. Lleras-Muney A. The Relationship Between Education and Adult Mortality in the United States. *Review of Economics Studies*. 2005;72:189-221.

70. The Consultative Group on Early Childhood Care and Development. What is ECCD? Available at: www.ecdgroup.com/what_is_ECCD.asp. Accessed March 11, 2002.

71. Olds D, Henderson CR Jr, Cole R, et al. Long-term effects of nurse home visitation on children's criminal and antisocial behavior: 15-year follow-up of a randomized trial. *JAMA*. 1998; 280;1238-1244.

72. Smedley B. Moving Beyond Access: Achieving Equity In State Health Care Reform. *Health Affairs*, March/April 2008. Vol 27, No. 2, pp 447-455

73. Prevention Institute. Health Equity Toolkit Key Informants Interview Synthesis document. 2008. Unpublished.

74. Institute of Medicine (2003). Smedley B, Stith A, Nelson A eds., *Unequal Treatment: Confronting Racial and Ethnic Disparities in Health Care*. Washington, D.C.: The National Academies Press; 2003.

75. Centers for Disease Control and Prevention. Health United States, 2007. Table 55. 2007. Available at: www.cdc.gov/nchs/data/hus/hus07.pdf

76. Centers for Disease Control and Prevention, National Center for Injury Prevention and Control. Webbased Injury Statistics Query and Reporting System (WISQARS). Feb 2006. Available at: www.cdc.gov/ncipc/wisqars.

77. Centers for Disease Control and Prevention, National Center for Injury Prevention and Control. Youth Violence. Available at: www.cdc.gov/ncipc/dvp/YV_DataSheet.pdf

78. United States Department of Transportation. National Highway Traffic Safety Administration. Race and Ethnicity in Fatal Motor Vehicle Traffic Crashes 1999 – 2004. May 2006. Available at: www.watchtheroad. org/809956.pdf. Accessed on April 3, 2009.

APPENDIX A

79. Centers for Disease Control and Prevention, National Center for Injury Prevention and Control. Webbased Injury Statistics Query and Reporting System (WISQARS). Available at: www.cdc.gov/ncipc/wisqars. Accessed on April 3, 2009.

80. National Center for Health Statistics. Health, United States, 2007 with Chartbook on Trends in the Health of Americans. Hyattsville, MD: U.S. Department of Health and Human Services; 2007.

81. National Minority Health Month Foundation. Study of Vital Statistics by ZIP Code Shows Health Disparities Affecting Minorities in the Treatment of Kidney and Cardiovascular Diseases. March 2007. Available at: www.rwjf.org/publichealth/product.jsp?id=18669. Accessed on April 3, 2009.

82. National Minority Health Month Foundation. Study of Vital Statistics by ZIP Code Shows Health Disparities Affecting Minorities in the Treatment of Kidney and Cardiovascular Diseases. March 2007. Available at: www.rwjf.org/publichealth/product.jsp?id=18669. Accessed on April 3, 2009.

83. National Health Interview Survey 2001-2005, available at www.cdc.gov/nchs/nhis.htm

84. National Institutes of Health. (2002). NIH's strategic research plan and budget to reduce and ultimately eliminate health disparities (Vol. I). Available at: http://ncmhd.nih.gov/our_programs/strategic/pubs/VolumeI_031003EDrev.pdf. Accessed on June 26, 2008.

85. Whitehead, M. The Concepts and Principles of Equity and Health. Copenhagen: WHO Regional Office for Europe. 1990. Available at: http://whqlibdoc.who.int/euro/-1993/EUR_ICP_RPD_414.pdf. Accessed on May 1, 2009.

86. Center for Medicare and Medicaid Services. Office of the Actuary, National Health Statistics Group.

87. Centers for Medicare and Medicaid Services, Office of the Actuary, National Health Statistics Group. 2006 National Health Care Expenditures Data. January 2008. Available at: www.cms.hhs.gov/nationalhealthexpenddata/01_overview.asp

88. Lee P and Paxman D, Reinventing Public Health. *Annual Review of Public Health*, 1997; Vol. 18: 1-35.

89. Prevention for a Healthier America: Investments in Disease Prevention Yield Significant Savings, Stronger Communities. Trust for America's Health, Prevention Institute, Urban Institute. 2008.

90. United States Breastfeeding Committee. Workplace breastfeeding support. Raleigh, NC: United States Breastfeeding Committee; 2002.

91. Brown MJ. Costs and benefits of enforcing housing policies to prevent childhood lead poisoning. *Medical Decision Making*. 2002;22:482-492.

92. Peters RM. The Negative Effect of the Clinical Model of "Health": Implications for Health Care Policy. *Journal of Health Care Finance*. 1998; 25:78-92.

93. Pincus T, Esther R, DeWalt DA, Callahan LF. Social Conditions and Self Management are more Powerful Determinants of Health than Access to Care. *Annals of Internal Medicine*. 1998; 129:406-411.

94. Institute of Medicine (2000). A social environmental approach to health and health interventions. In: Smedley BD, Syme SL, eds. *Promoting Health: Intervention Strategies from Social and Behavioral Research*. Washington, DC: National Academy of Sciences.

95. Smedley B, Stith A, Nelson A eds., *Unequal Treatment: Confronting Racial and Ethnic Disparities in Health Care*. Washington,D.C.:The National Academies Press; 2003: 5

96. The Commonwealth Fund. Medicaid Managed Care and Cultural Diversity in California. February 1999.Available at: www.cmwf.org/programs/minority/coye_culturaldiversity_311.asp#repfoot16. Accessed October 29, 2003.

97. Mokdad AH, Marks JS, Stroup DF, Gerberding JL. Actual causes of death in the United States, 2000. *JAMA*. 2004;291:1238-1245.

98. Davis R, Cook D, Cohen L. A community resilience approach to reducing ethnic and racial disparities in health. *American Journal of Public Health*. 2005;95:2168-73.

99. PolicyLink Health Disparities Team. Reducing Health Disparities Through a Focus on Communities. PolicyLink. November 2002.

100. Geronimus AT. Understanding and eliminating racial inequalities in women's health in the United States: the role of the weathering conceptual framework. *J Am Med Womens Assoc.* 2001;56:133-6, 149-50.

101. Mays VM, Cochran SD, Barnes NW. Race, Race-Based Discrimination, and Health Outcomes Among African Americans. *Annu Rev Psychol.* 2007; 58: 201-225.

102. Adler NE, Newman K. Socioeconomic disparities in health: pathways and policies. *Health Affairs.* 2002; 21(2): 60-76.

103. Lantz PM, House JS, Lepkowski JM, Williams DR, Mero RP, Chen J. Socioeconomic factors, health behaviors, and mortality. *JAMA.* 1998;279(21):1703-1708.

104. Smedley B, Jeffries M, Adelman L, Cheng J. Race, Racial Inequity and Health Inequities: Separating Myth from Fact. 2008. Available at: www.unnaturalcauses.org/assets/uploads/file/Race_Racial_Inequality_Health.pdf. Accessed on April 3, 2009.

105. Wandersman A, Nation M. Urban neighborhoods and mental health: psychological contributions to understanding toxicity, resilience, and interventions. *American Psychologist.* 1998;43:647-656.

106. Buka S. Results from the project on human development in Chicago neighborhoods. Presented at: 13th Annual California Conference on Childhood Injury Control; October 25-27, 1999; San Diego, CA.

107. Wilkenson R. Income inequality, social cohesion, and health: clarifying the theory – a reply to Muntaner and Lynch. International *Journal of Health Services.* 1999;29:525-545

108. Sampson RJ, Raudenbush SW, Earls F. Neighborhoods and violent crime: a multilevel study of collective efficacy. The American Association for the Advancement of Science. 1997;277(5328:15)918-924.

109. Pothukuchi K. Attracting Supermarkets to Inner-City Neighborhoods: Economic Development Outside the Box. *Economic Development Quarterly.* 2005; 19: 232-244.

110. Jackson RJ. Creating a Healthy Environment: The Impact of the Built Environment on Public Health. [Center for Disease Control and Prevention Website. Available at www.sprawlwatch.org. Accessed June 2000.

111. Centers for Disease Control and Prevention Public Health Practice Program Office. Principles of Community Engagement. Atlanta, GA, 1997.

112. Hancock, Trevor. "Healthy Communities must also be Sustainability Communities." *Public Health Reports.* Volume 115, March/April & May/June 2000.

113. Morland K, Wing S, Roux AD. The contextual effect of the local food environment on residents' diets: the atherosclerosis risk in communities study. *AJPH.* 2002;92(11):1761-1768.

114. Schmid TL, Pratt M, Howze E. Policy as intervention: environmental and policy approaches to the prevention of cardiovascular disease. *AJPH.* 1995;85(9): 1207-1211.

115. Coker A. Opportunities for Prevention: Addressing IPV in the Health Care Setting. *Family Violence Prevention and Health Practice.* 2005:1.

116. Sampselle M. The Role of Nursing in Preventing Violence against Women. *Journal Obstet Gynecol Neonatal Nurs.* 1991. 20: 281-7.

117. Schwartz IL. Sexual Violence against Women: Prevalence, Consequences, Societal Factors, and Prevention. *American Journal of Preventive Medicine.* 1991. 7(6): 262-373.

118. Coker A. Opportunities for Prevention: Addressing IPV in the Health Care Setting. *Family Violence Prevention and Health Practice.* 2005:1.

119. King MC. Changing Women's Lives: The Primary Prevention of Violence Against Women. AWHONN's Clinical Issues. 1993; 4 no 3.

120. Schwartz IL. Sexual Violence against Women: Prevalence, Consequences, Societal Factors, and Prevention. *American Journal of Preventive Medicine.* 1991. 7(6): 262-373.

APPENDIX A

121. Sampselle M. The Role of Nursing in Preventing Violence against Women. *Journal Obstet Gynecol Neonatal Nurs.* 1991. 20: 281-7.

122. Schwartz IL. Sexual Violence against Women: Prevalence, Consequences, Societal Factors, and Prevention. *American Journal of Preventive Medicine.* 1991. 7(6): 262-373.

123. King MC. Changing Women's Lives: The Primary Prevention of Violence Against Women. AWHONN's Clinical Issues. 1993; 4 no 3.

124. Sampselle M. The Role of Nursing in Preventing Violence against Women. *Journal Obstet Gynecol Neonatal Nurs.* 1991. 20: 281-7.

125. Schwartz IL. Sexual Violence against Women: Prevalence, Consequences, Societal Factors, and Prevention. *American Journal of Preventive Medicine.* 1991. 7(6): 262-373.

126. Sampselle M. The Role of Nursing in Preventing Violence against Women. *Journal Obstet Gynecol Neonatal Nurs.* 1991. 20: 281-7.

127. Schwartz IL. Sexual Violence against Women: Prevalence, Consequences, Societal Factors, and Prevention. *American Journal of Preventive Medicine.* 1991. 7(6): 262-373.

128. Schwartz IL. Sexual Violence against Women: Prevalence, Consequences, Societal Factors, and Prevention. *American Journal of Preventive Medicine.* 1991. 7(6): 262-373.

129. Sampselle M. The Role of Nursing in Preventing Violence against Women. *Journal Obstet Gynecol Neonatal Nurs.* 1991. 20: 281-7.

130. King MC. Changing Women's Lives: The Primary Prevention of Violence Against Women. AWHONN's Clinical Issues. 1993; 4 no 3.

131. King MC. Changing Women's Lives: The Primary Prevention of Violence Against Women. AWHONN's Clinical Issues. 1993; 4 no 3.

132. Prevention Institute. Reducing Healthcare Costs through Prevention. August 2007.

133. Prevention for a Healthier America: Investments in Disease Prevention Yield Significant Savings, Stronger Communities. Trust for America's Health, Prevention Institute, Urban Institute. 2008.

134. Smedley B. Moving Beyond Access: Achieving Equity In State Health Care Reform. *Health Affairs,* March/April 2008. Vol 27, No. 2, pp 447-455

135. Prevention Institute. Health Equity Toolkit Key Informants Interview Synthesis document. 2008. Unpublished.

136. Prevention Institute. Health Equity Toolkit Key Informants Interview Synthesis document. 2008. Unpublished.

137. Prevention Institute. Health Equity Toolkit Key Informants Interview Synthesis document. 2008. Unpublished.

138. PolicyLink. Available at: www.policylink.org/EDTK/Mapping/. Accessed on April 3, 2009.

139. Prevention Institute. Good Health Counts: A 21st Century Approach to Health and Community in California. November 2007.

140. Prevention Institute. Health Equity Toolkit Key Informants Interview Synthesis document. 2008. Unpublished.

B

Agenda

STATE AND LOCAL POLICY INITIATIVES TO REDUCE HEALTH DISPARITIES

Roundtable on the Promotion of Health Equity and the
Elimination of Health Disparities
Public Meeting
Cohosted by Allina Health Systems and United Health Foundation

Allina Commons–Minnesota Room
Minneapolis, MN

May 11, 2009

8:00 a.m	**WELCOME** *Dick Pettingill, Chief Executive Officer* *Allina Health System* *Nicole Lurie, Chair* *Institute of Medicine Roundtable on the Promotion of Health Equity and the Elimination of Health Disparities*
8:30 a.m.	**Presentation of Commissioned Paper** *Larry Cohen, Tony Iton, and Rachel Davis*
9:30 a.m.	**The Phillips-Powderhorn Experience and the Allina Backyard Project** **The Mayor's Perspective** *Minneapolis Mayor R. T. Rybak* **Historical Perspective** *Gordon Sprenger, former Allina Chief Executive Officer*

Current and Future Work with the Allina Backyard Project
Dick Pettingill

State Policy Efforts in Minnesota
Sanne Magnan, Commissioner
Minnesota State Health Department

11:30 a.m.   Audience Discussion and Questions

12:00 p.m.   WORKING LUNCH

1:00 p.m.   Health Disparities in Great Britain: Policy Solutions
Mildred Thompson (Roundtable Cochair), Session Chair

Introduction and Overview
Tom Granatir, Humana USA

National Support Teams: Emerging Themes from the Infant Mortality National Support Team Visits
Annette Williamson
Delivery Manager, Infant Mortality National Support Team
Department of Health, England

2:00 p.m.   Opportunities and Challenges: State Policies
Mildred Thompson, Introduction

Joel Weissman
Commonwealth of Massachusetts

2:30 p.m.   Break

2:45 p.m.   Reactor Panel
Mildred Thompson, Moderator

Winston Wong, Kaiser Permanente
Brian Smedley, Joint Center for Political and Economic Studies
Atum Azzahir, Phillips-Powderhorn Cultural Wellness Center

3:45 p.m.   Audience Discussion—State and Local Policies: What Works?

4:15 p.m.   **Wrap-up and Final Comments**
            Nicole Lurie

C

Speaker Biographical Sketches

Atum Azzahir founded the nonprofit Phillips-Powderhorn Cultural Wellness Center in 1996. It functions to provide a place where people can learn their own and each other's cultural traditions and health practices. The mission of the center is to unleash the power of citizens to heal themselves and to build community. A major goal of the center is to be the recognized authority on cultural approaches for preventing sickness and improving the health of individuals in a community context. Azzahir is the recipient of numerous awards, including the Salzburg Fellowship, Salzburg Seminars, Salzburg, Austria, 1993; Community Health Leadership Award, 1995, Robert Wood Johnson Foundation; Community Camara Award, Young Entrepreneurs Institute, 1999; Ruby H. Hughes Elder and Outstanding Citizenship Award, 2000; Race Unity Award of the BaHai Faith, 2000; recognition of outstanding community leadership, Leadership for a Changing World, 2002; and recognition as one of the 100 most influential health leaders in the *Minnesota Physician* August 2000 edition. Azzahir was also the recipient of the Leadership in Neighborhood grant to fund travel to Senegal and Benin, West Africa, Grenada in the West Indies, Jackson, Mississippi, and Cairo, Egypt, to study the role of elders in traditional African societies and compare them with the contemporary African elders in African American communities of the south. She has served on several key boards and committees, including the Minnesota Women's Fund, Chair, 1990–1992; National Network of Women's Fund, Chair, 1990–1993; The Sister Fund of New York, 1992; Medica Health Plans: Quality Committee, Community Affairs Committee, Executive Committee, 1997–2000; and HOPE Community Inc. Board of Directors, 1999–2001. Prior to founding the Phillips-Powderhorn Cultural Wellness Center, Azzahir served as vocational educational advisor, Minneapolis Technical Community College, 1981–1984; executive director, Harriet Tubman Women's Shelter, 1984–1989; and executive director, Way to Grow Youth Coordinating Board, 1989–1994. Azzahir currently serves on the Hennepin Health Systems Board as chair of the Governance and Mission Effectiveness Committee.

Larry Cohen, M.S.W., is founder and executive director of Prevention Institute, a nonprofit national center that moves beyond approaches that target individuals to create systematic, comprehensive strategies that alter the conditions that impact community health. With an emphasis on health equity, Cohen has led many successful public health efforts at the local, state, and federal levels focused on injury and violence prevention, mental health, traffic safety, healthy eating and physical activity and chronic disease prevention. Prior to founding Prevention Institute, he formed the first U.S. coalition to change tobacco policy and created the nation's first multicity smoking ban. He established the Food and Nutrition Policy Consortium and helped catalyze the nation's food labeling law.

Tom Granatir, A.M., serves as the Director of Public Health Initiatives at Humana, Inc. He has 20 years of experience in health policy at the American Hospital Association, the Health Research and Educational Trust, the Joint Commission on Accreditation of Healthcare Organizations, the Health and Medicine Policy Research Group, Humana Inc., and Humana Europe. His policy work has focused on patient-centered care, quality improvement, and public accountability in the mental health, hospital, long term care, and managed care sectors. He has served on the governing boards of the American Health Quality Association, the Institute for Safe Medication Practices, Bridges to Excellence, the National Association of Health Data Organizations, and Henry Booth House, a service agency for poor residents of Chicago. He has been an examiner for the Malcolm Baldridge National Quality Award Program and a member of the Health Policy Roundtable of the Michael Reese Health Trust. He currently serves on the Roundtable on the Promotion of Health Equity and the Elimination of Health Disparities of the Institute of Medicine of the National Academy of Sciences and is on the board of the Alliance to Make U.S. Healthiest.

Anthony Iton, M.D., J.D., M.P.H., is the Alameda County, California, Public Health Department director and health officer. Iton's primary interest is the health of disadvantaged populations and the contributions of race, class, wealth, education, geography, and employment to health status. He has asserted that in every public health area of endeavor, be it immunizations, chronic disease, HIV/AIDS, sexually transmitted diseases, obesity, or even disaster preparedness, local public health departments must recognize that they are confronted with the enduring consequences of structural poverty, institutional racism, and other forms of systemic injustice. He further asserts that the only sustainable approach to eliminating health inequities is through the design of intensive, multisectoral, place-based interventions that are specifically designed to identify existing assets and build social, political, and economic power among a critical mass of community residents in historically underresourced communities. Iton received his medical degree at Johns Hopkins Medical School and subsequently trained in internal medicine and preventive medicine at New York Hospital, Yale University, and the University of California, Berkeley, and is board certified in both specialties. He has also received a law degree and a master's of public health degree from the University of California, Berkeley, and is a member of the California Bar. In 2006, he was awarded the prestigious Milton and Ruth Roemer Prize for Creative Public Health Work, awarded by the American Public Health Association to a U.S. local health official in recognition of outstanding creative and innovative public health work.

Nicole Lurie, M.D., M.S.P.H., is a senior natural scientist and the Paul O'Neill Alcoa Professor of Health Policy at the RAND Corporation. She directs RAND's public health and preparedness work as well as RAND's Center for Population Health and Health Disparities. She has previously served in federal government, as Principal Deputy Assistant Secretary of Health in the U.S. Department of Health and Human Services; in state government, as medical advisor to the commissioner at the Minnesota Department of Health; and in academia, as professor in the University of Minnesota Schools of Medicine and Public Health. Lurie has a long history in the health services research field, primarily in the areas of access to and quality of care, managed care, mental health, prevention, public health infrastructure and preparedness, and health disparities. She attended college and medical school at the University of Pennsylvania and completed her residency and M.S.P.H. at the University of California, Los Angeles, where she was also a Robert Wood Johnson Foundation Clinical Scholar. She serves as senior editor for *Health Services Research* and has served on editorial boards and as a reviewer for numerous journals. She has served on the council and was president of the Society of General Internal Medicine, is currently on the board of directors for the Academy of Health Services Research, and has served on multiple other national committees. She is the recipient of numerous awards, including the Association for Health Services Research Young Investigator Award, the Nellie Westerman Prize for Research in Ethics, and the Heroine in Health Care Award, and is a member of the Institute of Medicine. In addition to her work in health services research and health policy, Lurie continues to practice clinical medicine in the health care safety net.

Sanne Magnan, M.D., Ph.D., was appointed Minnesota Commissioner of Health by Governor Tim Pawlenty on September 28, 2007. Magnan is responsible for directing the Minnesota Department of Health (MDH). MDH is the state's lead public health agency and is responsible for protecting, maintaining, and improving the health of all Minnesotans. The department has approximately 1,300 employees in the Twin Cities area and in seven offices in greater Minnesota. Prior to being appointed commissioner, Magnan served as president of the Institute for Clinical Systems Improvement (ICSI) in Bloomington, Minnesota. An independent, nonprofit organization, ICSI facilitates collaboration on health care quality improvement by medical groups, hospitals, and health plans that provide health care services to people who live and work in Minnesota and adjacent states. Magnan serves as a staff physician at the Tuberculosis Clinic at St. Paul-Ramsey County Department of Public Health and a clinical assistant professor of medicine at the University of Minnesota. She was named one of the 100 Influential Health Care Leaders by *Minnesota Physician* in 2004 and 2008. Magnan holds a medical degree and a doctorate in medicinal chemistry from the University of Minnesota. She earned her bachelor's degree in pharmacy from the University of North Carolina.

Richard "Dick" Pettingill, M.A., is chief executive officer of Minneapolis-based Allina Hospitals and Clinics, a nonprofit health care organization serving communities throughout Minnesota and western Wisconsin. Allina owns and operates hospitals, clinics, hospice services, pharmacies, medical equipment, and emergency medical transportation services. It employs approximately 22,000 people. Prior to joining Allina in 2002, Pettingill served for 6 years with Oakland, California-based Kaiser Permanente, one of the nation's largest health care systems. He was executive vice president and chief operating officer of Kaiser Foundation Health Plans and Hospitals, president and chief executive officer of Kaiser's California Division, and senior vice president/service area manager of Kaiser Foundation Health Plan and Hospitals. Before joining Kaiser Permanente, Pettingill served as president and chief executive officer of Camino Healthcare in Mountain View, California, and has held executive positions with El Camino Hospital and the El Camino Hospital District. He also served at Stanford University Hospital in Palo Alto, California, in several senior administrative roles. Pettingill's educational background includes a bachelor's degree in public administration from San Diego State University, San Diego, California, and a master's of arts degree in health care administration from San Jose State University. In 2001, he completed the Harvard Business School Executive

Leadership Program. Pettingill serves on the Allina Hospitals and Clinics board of directors. In March 2004, he joined the board of directors of Texas-based Tenet Healthcare Corporation, a publicly traded company.

R. T. Rybak was first elected mayor of Minneapolis in 2001 with his first run for public office and was just reelected to serve another term for the people of Minneapolis. Rybak has a broad background in business, journalism, and community activism. Prior to becoming mayor, Rybak was a business consultant, newspaper publisher, Downtown Council development director, and a reporter with the *Minneapolis Tribune*. As mayor, Rybak streamlined the city's economic development functions, created a $10 million housing trust fund, adopted the city's first Code of Ethics, and saved taxpayers millions by reducing $72 million of inherited debt with six balanced budgets in 4 years. Minneapolis now leads the state in affordable housing production, job creation, and the arts, with nearly $3 billion of development investment under way. Rybak is a lifelong Minneapolis resident and the son of a pharmacist in the Phillips-Powderhorn neighborhood. Rybak currently lives in the East Harriet neighborhood of Minneapolis with his wife, Megan, and their two children, Grace and Charlie. Professional history: reporter, *Star Tribune*, 1979–1986; development director, Downtown Council, 1986–1989; consultant, Eberhardt Development, 1989–1990; principal, R. T. Rybak Company (marketing consultant), 1990–1995; publisher, *Twin Cities Reader*, 1995–1997; vice president, Channel 4000, Internet Broadcasting, 1997–1999; principal, R. T. Rybak Company (Internet consultant), 1999–2001; and Minneapolis mayor, 2002–2005.

Brian D. Smedley, Ph.D., is vice president and director of the Health Policy Institute of the Joint Center for Political and Economic Studies in Washington, D.C. Formerly, Smedley was research director and cofounder of a communications, research, and policy organization, The Opportunity Agenda (www.opportunityagenda.org), whose mission is to build the national will to expand opportunity for all. Prior to helping launch The Opportunity Agenda, Smedley was a senior program officer in the Division of Health Sciences Policy of the Institute of Medicine (IOM), where he served as study director for studies that culminated in publication of the IOM reports *In the Nation's Compelling Interest: Ensuring Diversity in the Health Care Workforce* and *Unequal Treatment: Confronting Racial and Ethnic Disparities in Health Care*, among other reports on diversity in the health professions and minority health research policy. Smedley came to the IOM from the American Psychological Association (APA), where he worked on a wide range of social, health, and education policy topics in his capacity as Director for Public Interest Policy. Prior to working at the APA, Smedley served as a

Congressional Science Fellow in the office of Rep. Robert C. Scott (D-VA), sponsored by the American Association for the Advancement of Science. Among his awards and distinctions, in 2004 Smedley was honored by the Rainbow/PUSH coalition as a Health Trailblazer award winner, in 2002 he was awarded the Congressional Black Caucus Healthcare Hero award, and in August 2002 was awarded the Early Career Award for Distinguished Contributions to Psychology in the Public Interest by the APA.

Gordon M. Sprenger, M.H.A, is the former president and chief executive officer of Allina Health System. He was previously an executive for the HealthSpan Health Systems Corporation, Lifespan Inc., and Abbott Northwestern Hospital. Sprenger serves on the board of directors for the Joint Commission Resources and has held a number of other leadership positions with the Joint Commission. He holds a bachelor's degree from St. Olaf College and a master's in health administration from the University of Minnesota, where he also served as a faculty member until 2007.

Mildred Thompson, M.S.W., is the senior director and director of the PolicyLink Center for Health and Place, where she leads the work of the organization's heath team, participates in research focused on understanding community factors that impact health disparities, and identifies practice and policy changes needed to improve individual, family, and community health. She is also deputy director of the Robert Wood Johnson Foundation's Center to Prevent Childhood Obesity. Thompson has authored several reports and journal articles focused on reducing health disparities, increasing awareness about social determinants of health, and effective ways to impact policy change. Prior to joining PolicyLink, she was director of Community Health Services for the Alameda County, California, Public Health Department; Director of Healthy Start, a federal infant mortality reduction program; and director of San Antonio, Texas, Neighborhood Health Center. Thompson has degrees in nursing and psychology and a graduate degree in social work from New York University. She has also taught at Mills College and San Francisco State University and has worked as an organizational development consultant. Thompson is frequently sought for presentations and keynote addresses and serves on several boards and commissions, including The Zellerbach Family Foundation; cochair, the Institute of Medicine's Roundtable on the Promotion of Health Equity and the Elimination of Health Disparities; the California Health Policy Institute; and the Consortium to Lower Obesity in Chicago Children.

Joel S. Weissman, Ph.D., is on leave from Harvard Medical School while he serves as the Senior Health Policy Advisor to the Secretary of the Executive Office of Health and Human Services, Commonwealth of Massachusetts, and as professor of family and community medicine, University of Massachusetts Medical School. Among his responsibilities are to provide general policy guidance and to lead multipayer, multistakeholder health reforms in the areas of primary care, avoidable readmissions, health information technology, and disparities for vulnerable populations. At Harvard, Weissman holds joint faculty appointments at the Institute for Health Policy at Massachusetts General Hospital and at the Harvard School of Public Health. He has published over 100 peer-reviewed articles on the topics of quality and patient safety; racial-ethnic disparities; the uninsured; health care financing, including uncompensated care; drug policy; and academic-industry relationships in biomedical research. He is author (Arnold Epstein as coauthor) of the book *Falling Through the Safety Net: Insurance Status and Access to Care*, with a forward by Hillary Rodham Clinton. Weissman received his doctorate in health policy from the Pew Fellows Program at the Heller School, Brandeis University. He has led numerous federally funded studies, including those examining the relation of patient safety to hospital crowding, the reporting and disclosure of medical errors to patients, access to clinical trials by uninsured participants, E-prescribing in Massachusetts, and alternative scoring methods for pay for performance and was the lead evaluator for Consumer's Union Best Buy Drugs program. Weissman continues to serve as codirector of a course on health services research methods for the Program on Clinical Effectiveness at the Harvard School of Public Health, portions of which have been taught for the Singapore National Healthcare Group and the University of Puerto Rico.

Annette Williamson has undertaken the role of delivery manager for the Infant Mortality National Support Team since February 2009 within the Department of Health in the United Kingdom. Prior to her current role, she had 3 years' experience as a program manager within the Birmingham Health and Wellbeing Partnership with responsibility for the implementation of a multimillion-pound plan to reduce infant mortality within one of England's most deprived cities. Williamson has worked within the National Health Service for 30 years, the last 7 of them as an operational community manager and subsequently as a commissioner of Children and Young Peoples Services before joining the Birmingham Health and Wellbeing Partnership. Annette is by profession a registered general nurse, registered midwife, and registered health visitor; she holds a master's degree in primary health service management and was selected to participate in a King's Fund Leadership program, which included an international module.

Winston F. Wong, M.D., M.S., serves as medical director, Community Benefit, Kaiser Permanente, and Director of Disparities Improvement and Quality Initiatives. Kaiser Permanente is the nation's largest prepaid, multidisciplinary health care provider, with 8.7 million members, a physician group of 12,000, and 134,000 employees. Wong is responsible for developing partnerships with communities and agencies in advancing population management and evidence-based medicine, with a particular emphasis on safety net providers and the elimination of health disparities. A previous captain of the Commissioned Corp of the U.S. Public Health Service, Wong was awarded the Outstanding Service Medal while serving as both the chief medical officer for the Health Resources and Services Administration, Region IX, and its director of California Operations. Bilingual in Cantonese and Toisan dialects, Wong continues a small practice in family medicine at Asian Health Services in Oakland, California, where he previously served as medical director.